ADVANCED READING TECHNIQUES

ANGEL PATHS TAROT

JAN SHEPHERD

ANGEL PATHS

CONTENTS

CUPS

SWORDS

DISKS

ACKNOWLEDGMENTS

So here we are again, at that point where I look back across the period in which ART (as it has come to be known) was "birthing". This one has made its demands, and traversed a remarkable period in my life, suffering quite a few delays as a result.

In many respects, there's little variant here on the theme I played to this song when concluding the "Personal" special thanks. My trusty editor, Ellie, has been right there by my side every step of the way – that woman does the most remarkable job of cheering me on from the side-lines despite the fact that I am doubtless driving her quite mad at times. My animals work ceaselessly to ensure I keep my feet firmly on the ground, and impose some sort of routine into my days, at least where they are concerned. Visitors to the website, and to the Facebook page contact me with their feedback, their stories and their observations about my words. And the same is true of those people who have bought The 2nd Edition Guide to Tarot, and This Time It's Personal. It is quite humbling to discover how much my work helps along the way, and truly inspiring too. So grateful thanks to all of them. Amanda Wiebe did my images for me again, demonstrating once more her outstanding and visionary gift. She can be contacted at www.prodesignstudio.co.uk.

At the end of the thanks section in Personal I said these following words – and since I can think of no more fitting tribute to all of you, here they are again: I wish you well on your personal journeys, and trust that we will meet along the path, to sit down and share our experiences, our ups, our downs and our visions one with another. Light Bearers are the essence of hope. Never stop believing that each and every one of us can, and does, make a difference.

Thank you all. Each of you is precious.

Loadsa love

Jan Shepherd

www.angelpaths.com

November 2016

INTRODUCTION

There comes a point for the budding Tarot reader where they feel they have a fairly good grip on the meaning of each card. At this point, a new issue begins to emerge – how exactly do the cards relate to other cards? What kind of impact does the appearance of one card have on the one that follows it? And how do we make sense of what appear to be contradictions between cards in the same reading?

These sorts of questions yield some interesting answers when considered deeply. Cards do react to both amplify and diminish their neighbours. Often a reading will offer an overview when first considered, before the reading process itself begins. This overview is very useful to the reader because it presents a framework within which they can then work.

This book gives a comprehensive explanation of how cards can be read in relation to others. Most of the information here arises from my experience of reading various types of spread. Another important component to interpreting a spread effectively relies on a full understanding of the complexities of the position in which a card appears – but this is probably the topic of another book!

The Tarot is infinitely varied and extensive in the tales it can tell us of human life, and of spiritual development. Here I have attempted to capture some of the interactions that commonly arise in readings. However it is important to bear this in mind - just because I interpret a specific group in a specific fashion does not mean you cannot develop an extension of that understanding yourself. As your confidence and experience grow, it is important to allow yourself to learn from your own intuition and insight. I could probably write a ten-volume work on Tarot interactions and still not have run out of permutations. So use this book as a springboard into broader and more perceptive interpretations yourself.

Hopefully, at the very least, I will be able to offer you a starting point for learning to understand how one card can impact another, and how subtle nuances can appear when we have a broader understanding of similarities and conflicts between them.

Reading for Others

When you are learning to read the Tarot, there comes this point where you really need to spread your wings a little bit and start to look for willing "victims". These will usually start off being friends and relatives – and then friends of friends and relatives. There are some very important things to bear in mind when you reach this stage.

Doing a Tarot reading releases information that only resides in the subconscious mind. Hopefully by now you have already given yourself a fair number of frights along the way, by being stunningly and inexplicably accurate in readings you do for yourself. Just remember something – knowing things about another person that you have no rational way of knowing, is, at the very least, somewhat startling for your querent. Being able to accurately predict "what comes next" can be even more disconcerting – or even, downright frightening.

Whenever you exercise this skill for somebody who does NOT work to develop their own psychic abilities, you are in an exceedingly powerful position. You know the unknown. You "see" what is shrouded from their sight. Whatever you do, never ever forget this. It becomes increasingly important to carry this thought into every reading, the more efficient and accurate you become.

When you reach my level of experience, in the eyes of some people, you have achieved the level of a demi-god. Whatever you do, never ever fall for the illusion. You are as human and as fallible as the next person. Do not, under any circumstances, give in to the temptation to revel in that power – because if you do, for just one single minute, it WILL come back to bite you in the backside.

I have been read by readers who do the whole coin-tasselled headscarf, and magickal passes over the cards routine... and from the very second they start this rubbish I lose faith. What it tells me is that they do not respect the years and years of study and work they should have put in, in order to reach some level of expertise. Tarot-reading is NOT a mystical happening. It is the result of dedicated and often frustrating study and consideration.

When you start reading for others, you probably will still need all your reference sources, so be honest. Just remind your querent you are learning, and take the whole lot with you. There is nothing more frustrating to being a guinea pig than being told "I'll get back to you after I have done some research." You should KNOW if you need research to do an adequate reading.

Do not pander to your own ego by leaving the books and the laptop behind. Making reference does not mean you will not do an adequate reading, driven by your own intuition... it just means you are careful and respectful. And so you should be when dealing with somebody else's life.

One thing you should have learned, before you do readings for others, is that Tarot makes you think very hard about your approaches and attitudes to given areas of life. The cards, by their very nature, try to get the best out of you, and will do so for your querents also. Reading Tarot is much more than simply "looking into a crystal ball". It is driving the way you approach your life in the best possible way. You are not merely a Tarot reader... you are a Tarot counsellor. It is your job to express adequately how your querent can get the very best possible result from their life. If you need to, do some study on communicating with others in a fashion that supports and inspires them.

Another thing to be very aware of, when doing a reading, is that because of your position of remarkable authority and strength (whether you deserve that or not), what you say can sink deep into the subconscious of your querent. From there it is capable of emerging as a self- fulfilling prophecy which the querent themselves unconsciously realises into life. Tell a person "You are going to cheat on your husband" and you give them permission to do so. Far better to tell them they are approaching a situation which is going to provide temptation, which they would be better off side-stepping. Tell a querent "You are going to have a life-threatening illness" and there is a real danger they will allow a controllable health condition to descend into something lethal. More effective in this situation to impress upon them the importance of getting adequate medical advice in time. People on the receiving end of power relationships tend to be very impressionable. Mind your words. You might just kill somebody otherwise.

On a related topic, beware the power of hopes and wishes in your querent. If they select cards with a single-minded (or even obsessional) need for a given outcome, it is very possible they will skew results. Cards reflect the foremost pressing issues in a person's subconscious - sometimes they can simply reflect back precisely what the querent wants to hear. You should be able to "feel" this... such a reading feels empty somehow – there is nothing to reach for beyond the basic information. Ask them to redraw cards.

This leads me to two other topics which are "bees in my bonnet". When I taught small groups of people to read to a professional standard, I always told them "Do not go fishing for information." We have all been in this position – a reader looks for confirmation on every single point they make, studying our expressions, subliminal responses, and unconscious actions in order to glean information to push them forward. Well... look... if you have learned your cards properly THEY will tell you everything you need to know. Do not go "fishing" for more information. When you do this you confirm one single fact – you are not ready to read for others.

Then there are the querents who simply sit there stony-faced and utterly refuse to react. Now that is their right. It is their reading. If they then tell you that you are wrong, you have two options – draw a new set of cards (these will reiterate the original point if you were right in the first place) or simply admit you cannot read for the person concerned. Actually, as a professional reader, returning a person's cash or refusing to take it because "you could not read" tends to cause some extreme confusion in the querent. This is not necessarily desirable... but does weed out the people who are trying to get a reading for free.

When is it time to think about charging for readings? I am quite inflexible on this one. If you have learned under the tutelage of a watchful and experienced teacher, you will be ready to charge when they SAY you are. If you are learning under your own steam then there are certain criteria that you can evaluate to decide:

1. Can you describe a broad spectrum of meanings for each and every card in the deck without referring to other sources?
2. Can you randomly put together meanings for three cards if faced with twenty permutations?
3. Have you done more than a hundred readings for others where you have received positive feedback?

If the answer to all three is Yes, you are ready to contemplate going professional. And bear in mind... I said contemplate...

You will hear a lot of rubbish spoken about charging for this sort of service. Some people have an idea this is some great gift which fell upon your head from on high... but if you really ARE ready to read professionally the one thing you will know beyond a shadow of a doubt is this – there is no magick bullet to learning to read the cards accurately. It takes years of study. Just like any other profession in which you study and prepare, Tarot-reading is no different. You are entitled to be paid for a skill you have worked exceptionally hard to acquire.

Oh... and one last thing. When you DO start charging for readings, register with your relevant tax authority, and declare your income. You are dealing with the unseen and the unknown... make no mistake that tax officers are doing precisely the same when looking for dodgers ;-)

On Interpreting Difficult Readings

Anybody who reads for others will have encountered the kind of querent who says, just before the reading begins, "You won't tell me anything bad, will you?" I suppose the fear is natural enough... but there is only one ethical answer that can be given to a question like that – "If it's there, I'm going to read it for you. Leave now if you are not comfortable with that." It sounds brutal, I know – but there really is nothing else you can do.

None of us want to lay down a bad reading – for ourselves or for anybody else. Yet inevitably, this IS going to happen. It is important to think through our reactions, beliefs and feelings about this, so that when it happens, we know how to handle it. We need to develop strategies for coping with either receiving or conveying bad news.

One thing that is VERY important to recognise right at the beginning is that Tarot reading is not a precise science. You might be pretty sure Fred is seeing Irma without Hetty's knowledge... but there's no way the cards will show you that. What they will tell you is that Hetty needs to be watchful, because somebody around her is up to skulduggery. They will probably also indicate how this situation needs to be handled. We must therefore be wary of allowing our imaginations, our suspicions and our assumptions to run away with our interpretive skills.

This is important whether you are reading for yourself, or for somebody else. If you happen to be Hetty, doing a day reading for a general view, and you see some type of deception going on (Moon, perhaps, or Hanged Man, or even the Prince of Swords) beware of jumping to conclusions. Any apparent secrecy might be about something as innocent as planning your surprise birthday party next week. Daily, or even weekly readings tend to liberally use Major Arcana cards in a way that longer term readings do not. I have had the Tower, Death and the Devil come up in a 7-card spread to indicate a peculiarly difficult day. Had these cards appeared in a reading running for some months, I would have been seriously concerned. But because they appeared in a day reading, I expected (and got) a hard-fought breakthrough in personal work, and a near-quarrel with somebody I love, followed by some frustration that the row wasn't entirely resolved – not exactly what you would immediately imagine from this combination. However, I have to say when I saw the cards I felt an almost instinctual stab of fear... ;-)

How about when you are reading for another person? First and foremost you must remember that you have a very strong duty to serve highest principles when working with another person's future. When you present an individual with frightening, saddening or painful information, it is up to you to put that information across in the most empathetic fashion you can. Also, it is important to bear in mind that different people receive bad news in different ways – the person who appears perfectly equanimous may in fact be screaming inside. Equally the person who reacts sharply might not take in everything you have said after the initial shock.

When faced with having to tell somebody something bad, begin by explaining that whilst the cards are generally right in the information they give, that information is, by no means, set in stone. To a large extent we create our own future – some events can be altered, muted or outright avoided by proper handling of knowledge gained through the cards.

When you tell your querent what you have found, do not allow yourself to be pinned down to possible scenarios unless you are absolutely certain that they could be right. And even so, underline the idea that you are trying to illustrate by example, not offering an absolute prediction. Your querent knows a great deal more about what is going on in their lives than you do – if a particular situation is bothering them, sometimes it is tempting to try to bend the known difficulty to fit the cards, rather than contemplate a new issue. Give only the information you feel comfortable with.

Try to stress the solutions offered by the cards – and if the end result looks to be a good one, then emphasise this, so that the querent has light at the end of the tunnel. It is quite rare for a spread to reveal a really awkward issue and not present possibilities of lessening it, or dealing with its impact.

And what if you see an event which really is extremely nasty and unpleasant? What if this appears to be imposed from outside, and therefore largely beyond your querent's control? I have, over the years, read rape, violent attack, sudden death and global tragedy which has a personal implication for my querent. As I have turned over the cards in a reading, I have developed the sickening certainty in the pit of my stomach that something absolutely dreadful was going to happen. This has happened both in personal readings (I tend most usually to get the global tragedy breakthrough in my own cards) and in readings for clients.

On every occasion I have thought carefully about my personal gut reaction to the reading, then tried to pull back and look for an objective standpoint. Whilst not dismissing my own feelings, I have then attempted to interpret the reading as evenly as possible. Where danger is apparent, I indicate this to the querent, and advise methods of protection or defence. This is a delicate balance – if you see the possibility of violent attack, you want your querent to listen to you. But it is non-constructive to frighten them so badly they feel helpless and unable to take care of themselves. Read the section on self-fulfilling prophecies in "Reading for Others" again to understand more about this. The single most important issue about offering a reading like this is to ensure that your querent knows you are concerned for them – though not happy to be the messenger on this occasion. Ensure that your interest in their well-being shows. But be careful not to give them a guilt-trip for having brought you the reading ;-)

You can, if you are thoughtful enough, be very instrumental in contributing to a person's safety. Many years ago, a reading I did for a young woman clearly indicated some kind of sudden and vicious attack. The run of cards was: 3 of Disks (going about her everyday business), Tower, Devil, 9 of Swords, 7 of Cups, 10 of Swords, Knight of Swords (among others which I don't now remember). She sat silently throughout the reading, and at the end she said "I see. You think I am liable to be attacked soon then?" With some trepidation I confirmed this. She then told me she was a student at university, and that there had been a series of sexual assaults on female students. She went away, having decided that she would not move around the campus alone – instead always ensuring she was with trusted colleagues or friends. She rang me a while later to say that she had not been attacked, and that the perpetrator had now been caught – but not before 4 other lone women had been subject to attack.

Interpreting tough readings is never something that we would volunteer for. But when we are faced with one, we do have to have the integrity, strength and sincerity to tell it like it is. This takes courage, self-trust and self-belief. Never ever forget the importance and power inherent in your own words.

Dignifications and Reversals

Whether or not to read card reversals in a spread is a vexing and often confusing question. There are as many arguments for as there are against. Just to confound things yet more, there are no commonly held beliefs about exactly what constitutes a reversed interpretation. Some users of the reversal method quite literally turn an upright card meaning on its head, so a positive upright card becomes a negative in the process of its reversal. Other readers extrapolate what might be construed as the "bad" end of an interpretation and apply that when a card presents reversed. And there are even certain respected commentators who present completely unrelated meanings to a reversed card which have little to do with the upright conno-tations.

Add to all this the fact that not all tarot readers return all cards in their deck to an upright position after doing a reading, and you have opened before you the kind of can of worms it is nearly impossible to sort out, especially for a relative novice.

My personal preference is NOT to read reversals. After every reading I do, I shuffle my deck to clear it of any residual influence, and in so doing take the opportunity to return any inadvertently reversed cards to their upright position. In this way I guarantee to myself that when I return to use that deck again it is fundamentally "clean" of any earlier use. So for me if a card DOES reverse in a reading at least I know it belongs to that shuffle and not to some random cut I did a year ago last Wednesday.

Why do I choose not to read reversals? Well, when I view a tarot card I see its interpretation as one which exists within a kind of continuum. For example, the Ace of Cups refers, at its core, to pure, unsullied and freely expressed feelings of love and joy, usually (but not always) centring upon another person. So here we see love affairs, deep surging emotions, and glorious expression of powerful feelings. However, it's an Ace. Aces always indicate (by their very nature) beginnings. So for this reason this Ace can show the heady beginning of a true love partnership. It can also point to the conception of a joyously contemplated child. But – and this is very important – Cups also relate to the powerful and unique expressions of creativity which exist deep within us. So if my querent is, for example, an artist, this Ace might appear to indicate the beginning of a master work. If a person has a deep longing to do a specific job or task, this Ace could indicate that beginning. I could continue with examples here for quite some time... but no doubt you already get the idea.

So, one single card can present us with a very broad-sweeping array of different meanings, each of which may be valid in a specific circumstance. Why would we then say "And then if it is reversed this bad bit here applies"? Surely that over-simplifies what should be an expansive range of knowledge about that single symbol? And anyhow, within that wide swathe of reference we might also easily include less important, or less positive perspectives. For example, that Ace can sometimes indicate the kind of person is falls in love with the idea of love, who is incapable of rooting this vast emotion into the nuts and bolts of everyday life. So more negative or "lesser" aspects of the card can emerge anyway.

Of course, all this poses one really crucial question – how on earth do we work out which aspect of the presented card actually demonstrates now? I think this is possibly the single most intimidating aspect of Tarot for the novice. And, fascinatingly, it is also an aspect which keeps me endlessly entranced by the all-encompassing reach of this chosen medium. I have not yet finished studying the Tarot... and I doubt I ever will.

But – to try to begin to answer that crucial question – well, it's complicated! For one thing, as I have mentioned before, the position in which the card presents is very important in terms of our approach to its interpretation. A card referring to events in the past will often be much more finite and clear-cut than one presenting in a future position. Furthermore, the aspect of the card that we select as relevant also depends upon whether a position is inward-facing or outward-facing – hopes and fears is an obvious example of an inward-facing position, whereas outside influences is clearly outward-facing.

Then the context in which a specific card is presented in a reading, in relation to the cards which surround it, is also very relevant. An Ace of Cups surrounded by high Swords is not describing a happy situation. But that same Ace surround by loving and intimate Cups and Majors presents a very rosy picture indeed. And then yet again, this selfsame card wrapped about with Disks or Wands might point much more to the beginning of a heartfelt and emotionally powered project.

And at this point the novice throws all their cards into the air shouting "HELP!"

Forgive me for pausing to chuckle – I know that feeling very well. However there is one particular system that I have applied from the very early days of reading cards – that of dignifications. This means that some cards are strengthened toward a positive interpretation (dignified) by the appearance of some others; conversely, another set of neighbouring cards may weaken (ill-dignify) the initial card toward the negative. Working out what applies where is a matter of learning, and experience, but there are some basic rules of thumb we can apply, especially to the Minor Suits.

Once you get the hang of incorporating dignifications, they become almost second nature, especially as your grasp of specific cards also broadens. These ideas will extend the subtlety and "touch" of your reading enormously, so it's worth grappling with the concepts. But be warned – at first sight, the principle of dignification looks horribly complex. Don't give up if you find what comes next hard to get hold of in the first place. I'll suggest to you some methods of trying to apply the ideas outlined here after I have thrown the raw concepts at you!

In your deck you will have Wands, Cups, Swords and Disks (or their equivalents). Each of these is applied to a given Elemental force from which its meaning and sphere of influence flows, thereby creating the overall "feel" of a given Suit. For example, under most circumstances the Tarot Suit of Wands is attributed to the Element of Fire; Cups to Water; Swords to Air; and Disks to Earth. There can be variants to this system – but here, for the sake of sparing your brain any more boggle-time, I will stick with these.

These Elements are either active or passive in nature. Wands and Swords are active Suits; Cups and Disks are passive Suits. Suits of common nature are inimical to each other – they argue one way or another. You might find it easiest to remember this bit if you think about what happens when you mix Elements – add Air to Fire to create a possible conflagration; add Water to Earth and you make mud. Each of the Elements is also directly balanced against its opposing Element – hence Wands (Fire) are balanced or "dignified" by Disks (Earth); Swords (Air) are friendly with (or dignified by) Cups (Water).

Mind you, just to confuse us yet further there is a sub-text here – Fire cannot burn without Air; Water is completely uncontained without Earth. So, whilst the actives and passives tend to "argue" with their closest relatives, they are also intimately inter-dependent.

Even more fascinating is what happens when we contrast the Elements against their opposite number... Earth extinguishes fire, but fire burns safely upon it – and to some extent requires material from the Element of Earth for its ability to burn in the first place. Air and Water are also irretrievably linked – all water contains air. If there is only a little air in the water it becomes fetid and stagnant. Vapour, in many cases, requires a combination of air and water. If you think about this you are likely to find a myriad of other circumstances in which these four basic Elements are interlinked and interdependent – so it is with the Suits of Tarot.

However, for our purposes, I am going to leave this enthralling tangle here and move on to numbers – for these too introduce dignification and ill-dignification.

The Ace and the 10 of any Suit will dignify each other – the beginning and the end. The 3, 6, and 9 of any Suit will dignify one another (or at least create a continuum) – this is because each number represents a stage of completion, with 9 being the pinnacle. 2, 4, and 8 dignify each other because they relate to the concept of expansion, with the 8 marking infinity. In both of these examples the middle card represents a point of pivot between the extremes indicated by the first and third.

Just as some numbers strengthen others, so do other combinations tend to weaken their neighbours. 3s tend to "clang" against 5s, and 4s argue with 7s. Also this kind of application can be carried across Suits - you might lay a reading with a preponderance of certain numbers but spread across the Elements – 3 of Cups, 2 of Wands, 5 of Swords is an example of arguments everywhere, for example. Even though the 2 and the 3 are relatively "good" cards, the 5 introduces a hint that all is not well in the balance struck between those two cards... so for example you might read this as a happy and contented period where you feel in control and settled, yet there is something rumbling beneath the surface which may or may not be pinned down somewhere else in the reading. And of course before being certain of your interpretation you would also need to take into account positioning... if those cards appeared in a "past present future" spread then they would assume a much more unstable tone.

Now there is every possibility that at this stage your brain is begging for mercy... so let me suggest a method of learning how to apply this now in readings. Lay down your spread and look primarily at the similarities and differences in the cards you see (this is why I do not like the "reveal one card at a time" method). Are there a lot of Cups? Then it is probably an emotionally based reading. Are there a couple of high Swords? Then there's trouble somewhere in the mix. Here you'd revert to positions briefly to get a feeling for where that trouble belongs – is it past? Or still to come? However in the scheme of things Swords and Cups do tend to cover some shared ground... so despite potential trouble, there's a kind of basic logic to the reading at first glance.

You can apply this sort of "snapshot" glance to all the Minors. One brief check will give you a frame of reference in terms of what area of life it applies to. Work first purely with the Suits in broad sweeps. Go back and read over "The Elements" article which is available both in the Angel Paths Guide to the Tarot and on the Angel Paths website.

When you are in a period of contemplation about Tarot, try taking cards from "friendly" Suits and thinking about how they interact together. You will begin to build your own associations and links here. Then repeat the exercise with cards from "argumentative" Suits and do the same. Take it very slowly. Building those personal leaps of understanding and intuition makes an essential contribution to your eventual quality as a Tarot reader. Take it from me – you will never ever STOP building links, no matter how long you study.

Give yourself plenty of time to come to an inner understanding of the Elements. Then start in on the numbers. Read the article "Tarot and Numbers" – again available in the Guide and here on the website. And then use the same steady process of familiarising yourself, stage by stage, with how the numbers themselves interact. You will already have a basic understanding of the Elemental effect by then.

You might well ask "Yes but what about the Majors?" Ah – well therein lies an entire separate book again.

So dignification is certainly a complex matter to get to grips with, but maybe you now see why I feel reversals are something of a blunt object. Nothing in Tarot is quite that simple. Whether you decide to use reversals, or dignifications, or nothing at all, is as ever, your decision in the end. But it is well worth playing with this approach if only to get a feel of how it can enhance your understanding of the cards, and the delicate dance they perform when laid down in a reading.

THE MAJOR ARCANA

THE FOOL

As the first card of the deck, the Fool represents beginnings. This effect is strengthened if he appears with Aces, and the suit of the Ace will direct your attention to the appropriate area of life.

He also indicates the willingness to take risks, so sometimes he will appear with cards like the 7 and 9 of Wands, showing that inner strength is needed in order to move forward. This interpretation would also apply if he appeared with Lust.

With the Sun, you would expect great rewards for the person willing to trust to life and follow their dreams. With the Universe you would expect a given phase or journey to have come to a point of natural conclusion.

Thoth Tarot

However his aspect of rashness is underlined when he appears with the Devil or the Tower. In these cases you would need to seek out cards which will identify exactly what the potential problems may be, and how they could be avoided. For example, the 7 of Swords suggests an internal problem – a sense that nothing can be done to change existing conditions. The 10 of Wands might indicate that a blockage or obstacle needs to be carefully considered, and swift action may be inadvisable. Caution would probably be the watch-word here.

With the Star, the Fool is a very bright card indeed, indicating that your querent is aligned with Universal power and has great ability to influence their life. With Fortune, you can be assured that risks will pay off. With Art (Temperance) some care is needed to ensure that everything is in balance. This would also be the case if the Fool appeared with the Chariot – here careful preparation would be important.

THE MAGUS

Thoth Tarot

Have you ever contemplated that part of you which is represented by this powerful card? It exists within each and every one of us... the driving desire to create what we need in our lives. Sometimes we dissipate its power in daydreams, or unfocussed imaginings. And it is an unfortunate fact that even when we do manage to focus sufficiently, it will often be upon negative outcomes that we centre our energies. It is worth asking yourself how often you end up seeing your worst fear come true, and how often your wildest dreams emerge into reality – if there's an imbalance in results, the chances are you are focussing your power on the wrong thing.

When the Magus appears in a reading, he will signify one of two things – an observation on our own position and power in that particular moment, or an external force which is having profound effect.

Look first at placement to work out which of these alternatives he indicates. In personal reference positions (your view of a topic, your hopes and fears, what you can do, whether there is an action you can take) he will indicate that your own Will, your own power and your own action are paramount. The card will come up to mark periods where your personal focus is such that you can make a difference. Look for the Aeon, Art and the Aces nearby to reinforce this view. The appearance of the Hermit might suggest that you are holding back too much, as would cards like the 4, 7 or 8 of Wands.

If the Magus appears in this context backed, for instance, by the Sun or the Chariot you could feel confident that your actions will be beneficial and effective. The 7 of Swords would suggest that you are getting in your own way, as would the 10 of Wands.

When he appears in positions which are more external to self in a reading – past events, immediate future events, external influences, you would be as well to consider whether you are looking at an actual person represented by the card. This would be emphasised if the reading also contained cards such as the Knight/King of Cups or Swords (both aspects of the Magus).

If the cards around it indicate that the Magus does represent a person, it is a good thing to remember that whilst men indicated by the Magus can be charming, fascinating, and interesting, they are often fundamentally very selfish individuals – they run strong personal agendas and have clear ideas of what they want to get out of given situations. For this reason they can sometimes be tricky to deal with. Watch out particularly if the Moon shows – there would be an implication of illusion here. Look out also for the 7 of Cups, or the Devil – the Magus has a way of tempting us to do things we would normally not even consider.

If, however, you find a 'person' Magus surrounded by cards such as the Priestess, the Star, Fortune, good Wands or solid Disks, expect him to introduce a new perspective which allows you to make good progress toward your personal goals. In this case he will often be a breath of fresh air that assists you in finding new solutions to old problems.

THE PRIESTESS

In traditional decks this card was known as the Papess – female pope – perhaps originally indicating the leader of the community of female priests we would now refer to as nuns. This gradual shift of emphasis has led to the shrouding of the High Priestess's significance when we attempt to read her in a spread. For many readers she remains either a shadowy figure who defies interpretation, or as an indication that intuition and the hidden senses are at work. Whilst this interpretation is valid, to some extent, it misses the deepest mysteries of this card, which can often lead to misunderstanding or lack of depth when reading the Priestess.

Thoth Tarot

Priestesses had, for many hundreds of years, a clearly defined and individuated role in society. In my opinion, it is partially the loss of this understanding that leads to confusion and frustration around womanhood in our modern-day society. The priestess was a complex being – she possessed a knowingness borne of harmony with all that is – a mysterious and barely half-understood knowledge of the might of the Goddess.

The God had his context here both as consort and offspring. She nourished and protected, murdered and resurrected, sacrificed and slaughtered. The Goddess was the silent pivot around which all else moved. And the priestess was Her handmaiden – charged to bring her influence to the world of men (and women ;-)

The Priestess then became not only teacher of matters of faith and trust, but also provider of healing, nurture and day to day protection. Life itself was her realm – its living, its dying, and all in-between.

The High Priestess has a certain affinity with the Magician – they are considered balanced counterparts, interlinked polarities which each reflect one side of a coin. However her truest affinity is with the Hierophant (originally the Pope in traditional decks). These two cards represent the highest concept of the God or Goddess's representative in the community. The Hierophant is charged with the transference of knowledge, the process of instructing the community in matters spiritual and ethical. The High Priestess is charged with the job of developing the hidden mind in order that it will attain a level allowing it to perceive god/dess in their entirety.

So (to get back to the point) when the High Priestess appears in a reading, be alert for indications that you need to read to a vastly deeper level of spirituality than usual. Cards which will emphasise this include the Chariot, the Moon, Art (Temperance) and the Star. Sometimes the Hermit may also appear. If you see cards like this grouped in a reading, be aware that you need to read far beyond the mundane level. You are reaching into the realms of psychism, spirit and revelation here.

Be prepared to interpret all other cards in the reading from this perspective. Cups, for instance, will transform into their most spiritual context – so the Ace would indicate an experience which might indicate ecstatic union with the High Powers. The 10 could point to completion of a stage in the spiritual quest, with its concomitant sense of ease and replenishment. The 5 may show that the querent is disappointed by the results of their current explorations.

Disks would shift in focus to the ways in which the querent earths the new knowledge they are acquiring – how they realise this into daily life. The 2 would show marked changes in the accepted order that things occur on a material level. The 6 would indicate a sense of radiating spiritual growth into life and attracting good energy as a result. The 9 would suggest a willingness in the querent to share their newfound wisdom with others, and the energy exchanges that this would create.

With Wands we look toward the active and directed movement toward greater spiritual understanding – the drive that powers this hunger. The Ace would show a fierce yearning for growth. The 4 would indicate that one stage of development has been completed. The 10 would point to areas of blockage in the quest.

And Swords, as the cardinal element, would be deeply significant if you were reading at this level. This suit is about our relationship to our beliefs, our thought processes, our inner and outer perceptions. It deals with communication at all levels, and in this context most particularly, with the unseen forces of life. It also deals with our responses to our own feelings, in part at an intellectual level, but also at the level of spirit.

Have you ever, when deeply embedded in pain, confusion and unhappiness, had a moment of clarity where you seem able to view yourself from a distance, dispassionately? Those people who have had this happen to them often describe their perception of their 'other' self as a little pathetic... a soul wallowing in pain, when they could be utilising all their power, focussing their pain, in order to get where they want to be. Of course, such a perception doesn't always help when you then belly-flop back into the mess. But if you can hold that high perspective for just long enough, it is usually enough to galvanise you into affirmative action, and throw you forward toward the rest of your life. And often later, with the wisdom of hindsight, you will look back at that tortured soul and wonder... then bless the lesson you learned from that sadness and move on.

THE EMPRESS

Thoth Tarot

This card always brings love into a reading when it appears – timeless, all-encompassing love, at its highest level. The Empress also talks about strength and female power.

For reading purposes, it is important to define whether the Empress represents a person or an effect. This can normally be decided by looking at the cards that surround it.

The Empress has a strong allegiance with the Queen courts. They are her manifestation as women. When you cast a Queen coupled with the Empress you will often be looking at the core of the woman in question. Mostly this will lead to a positive interpretation – Queen of Wands/Empress will suggest a woman who is deeply passionate about life, dynamic and determined; Queen of Disks/Empress emphasises the 'Earth Mother' aspect of this card, so can indicate fertility, and possibly childbirth; Queen of Swords/Empress combination can be a little more sticky – the Queen of Swords is an intellectual, with piercing clarity, whereas the Empress is instinctual, driven by her feelings; Queen of Cups/Empress can be a little over-indulgent and impractical, though with supporting good Cups would indicate very deep love and warmth.

When the Empress appears in the same reading as the Emperor you will usually be viewing people again. This pairing is one of the archetypal couples of the Major Arcana – the other being the High Priestess/Magician combination. Each of these produces what could be defined as the 'perfect' couple, and should be interpreted as such so long as other cards support that analysis. However if you get either pair turning up with negative cards surrounding them, you are most likely reading a situation which looked at the outset to be a perfect match, but which time proves to be the exact opposite.

When the Empress represents an effect, rather than a person, you'll often find a fair number of Wands and Disks around too. One particular combination to look out for is the Empress with the Ace of Wands – this very often indicates the beginning of new life – so childbirth or radical changes of direction. When you see the Empress with the Ace of Cups, the effect is slightly different – it can often show the beginning of an enduring and long-lasting relationship.

Whenever she appears she reminds us that love, offered freely, can change the world. She brings in a passionate and powerful lust for life (so she's particularly important when Lust or Strength also appears) which allows us to engage in detail with everything that is happening around us.

THE EMPEROR

This is one of the Major Arcana cards that can represent an influential person in the querent's life. In this case, he will indicate a powerful and dynamic man, with considerable power. When he does appear to show a person, do not be surprised to also find the Wand males appearing – these will often be slightly different views of the same man. If he appears with cards like the Empress, you are probably dealing with his strong connections to home and family life.

When this card appears to indicate an event, rather than a person, he tends to be a little more difficult to read. The Emperor encapsulates the concept of the Father – so he will come up to show father figures, or the need for them in life – look for cards such as damaged Cups to identify whether it is the need for a strong male figure which is indicated.

Thoth Tarot

He will also sometimes represent leadership qualities, and then the reading might be an instruction to the querent to be strong and decisive. This would be strengthened by cards like the 3 of Swords or the 7 of Swords.

With any Ace, the Emperor becomes an encouragement to take action – new projects are beginning, life changes are taking place and the most important thing for the querent is that they are willing to engage completely with what is happening around them. If he appears with the Ace of Disks or Wands the chances are that changes are taking place in the career field. With the Ace of Cups, it is more likely that personal areas of life need attention. With the Ace of Swords the concept of decision making is even more strongly underlined.

Another combination in which the Emperor can make a welcome and helpful appearance is where forceful Wands are flowing strongly in a reading. Wand energy can become quite unruly, with control being surrendered to recklessness, all caution and foresight thrown to the winds. The pure self-discipline of the Emperor tempers this rowdy effect, allowing us to harness and direct that fiery force into much more creative and productive channels.

Where the Emperor appears with the Devil, confusion can occur – this combination is often interpreted quite negatively. However, negativity is not always the primary influence when these cards appear together – the Devil and the Emperor both relate to underpinning issues like male sexuality, and masculinity. The two cards together can often indicate that inhibitions need to be shed and the male aspect of a man liberated. Look for cards like the Sun, Adjustment or low Wands to confirm this meaning.

THE HIEROPHANT

Thoth Tarot

This card tends to be one of those for which some readers have a blind spot. That blind spot sometimes results from its traditional representation as The Pope. The Pope is, of course, the titular incarnate leader of the Catholic church. The Archbishop of Canterbury takes up this role for the Anglican church. But such secular interpretations are a misunderstanding of the Hierophant's role in the Tarot. It is true that he stands for the most exalted religious leader of a given belief or tradition, but his function is not limited by a specific religious view – rather he is ALL leaders of ALL faiths. If the reader has a particular area in which they invest their personal beliefs then this will represent Thoth to an advocate of the Egyptian Mysteries, The Dalai Lama to a Buddhist, Mohammed to a Muslim, and so on. You will notice that in many of these examples the leader in question is no longer incarnate – but that leader's philosophies, approaches and interpretations will carry weight for the priest or adherent of that particular faith system.

As a singular "pillar" of a faith, the Hierophant carries with him (or her) the traditional values and credo of that faith. He or she must act in a fashion that attempts to live out the values of that faith into life and in so doing, provide an example to his/her priest/esses in a coherent and replicable fashion. He or she acts as the beacon which guides others forward.

The card also picks up on themes of inner belief, of the application of the Will of Gods, of the ability of the ordinary person to bring their life more closely into line with their faith.

The Hierophant exists in the space between men and gods, and in one sense is a messenger, carrying both the pleas and prayers of man to the gods, and dispensing and disseminating the Will of gods to men. In this way, he is a go-between – a bridge between beings. At his best he is wholly objective. He sees all points of view, and can set these against a background of acceptable living.

In practical terms, when this card appears in a reading the very first thing we need to take on board is that, one way or another, there is a very strong spiritual element to the spread. You would be surprised how rarely this does card appear in fact – that is because the circumstances which call him forth are usually out of the ordinary.

It is important to look for the two other powerful teaching Arcana amongst the cards – The Magus, or the Priestess. Each introduces a slightly different element. The Magus suggests that action is imperative in a given situation – and action which directly complies with the conscience of the querent. The Priestess suggests that there is teaching available which applies to a given situation, and which is only available from a higher source. If you find either of these in a reading along with the Hierophant, that reading needs treating with extreme care, for the gods are abroad and watching events.

If the Hierophant appears with the Tower then we know that a corrective action is imminent, and will be delivered by the gods themselves.

With Aces we must always turn to the highest spiritual level of interpretation when the Hierophant also appears; with Art or Adjustment there is a very strong chance that the aspect of the Hierophant that relates directly to spiritual Law will be invoked.

One interesting combination that will sometimes – though rarely – turn up is that of the Hierophant with the Hermit – here we are advised to turn to the Hiero within to find the answers we seek to pressing questions. With the Hanged Man he tends to revert most closely to his position "between the worlds" so to speak – we are awaiting enlightenment. With the Universe he indicates a final and just resolution to a difficult problem. As a living Hierophant, he will usually present as a Sword Court – this is where the insight and quicksilver thinking of the Sword comes into its own.

It is worth investing a good deal of effort into truly understanding the appearance of the Hierophant in readings, for it always presents a momentous challenge.

THE LOVERS

This card can be trickier to read than it may at first seem – the undercurrents within it that talk about aspects of self-love and respect can tend to confuse, until the reader gets to grips with the deeper meanings of the card.

For instance, what happens when this card comes up with the Moon, the Chariot, the Hermit, the Hanged Man – and not another person in sight? What happens when Art is crossed by the Lovers and there is no sign of a relationship? What does it mean when the High Priestess comes up in close proximity to the Lovers? These are all examples of times when you will be examining your querent's inner relationship with themselves. The preponderance of Major

Thoth Tarot

Arcana cards here appear because self-development is regarded as one of the most important processes of Tarot. So times when we draw close to the essence of ourselves, and consider deeply the relationship we have with the furthest regions of ourselves, are always momentous.

These are times when we can make massive steps forward... or alternatively, fail ourselves quite outstandingly. When you feel you are reading a period like this, ensure that you look for cards which indicate the natural outcome of events.

The 2 or 6 of Cups, the 6 of Swords, or the 9 or 10 of Cups would all indicate that we could use the period to our advantage and gain dramatically as a result. The 7, 9 or 10 of Swords, the 10 of Wands or the 5 of Disks would show that we might tend to shy away from our own personal reality. If the latter is indicated, look again for cards which indicate why we would choose to do this, and guidance for how to meet our fears and look them in the eye.

When the Lovers appears with cards like the Emperor and Empress, we are examining periods of mutually satisfying relationships with others - remember, the Emperor and Empress are often considered to be the couple showing on the Lovers card, the true alchemical union which rejuvenates the world. With the Ace of Cups, this card may show the beginning of a lasting relationship. With the 3 of Cups a marriage or other major step forward could be indicated. Note that, in these days of more flexibility within human relationships, the moment of commitment could mark where a couple move in together, or where they decide to have a child, as readily as marriage.

Another aspect of the Lovers is that sometimes it points to the necessity to make an important decision – often that a major choice needs to be made. Where this occurs with the 3 of Swords, there is a great deal of uncertainty – look for the 2 of Swords or the 6 of Swords to see whether satisfactory resolution can be found. The Hanged Man could show that the querent is dithering rather than making up their mind. The Ace of Swords could indicate sudden clarity and action.

The Lovers will also come up to represent long term and happy relationships – again often with the Emperor and Empress. Look for cards like the Star or Fortune to indicate continuing contentment.

THE CHARIOT

Thoth Tarot

The Chariot will always be a welcome arrival in a Tarot card reading – it symbolises problems and obstacles overcome, battles won and conflict finally resolved. Remember, when you see this card, that in some ways it is also a preparatory card, pointing out that you might have won the battle, but the peace has yet to be established. It is a card which tells us to be exceptionally careful in paying attention to detail.

When this card appears with the Sun or the Star, you are surveying a crucially important and fruitful time for your querent – this is emphasised even more if you get cards like the Wheel of Fortune, 6 of Disks or Wands coming up afterwards. These will indicate success of enterprises bringing growth and abundance.

The Chariot is also quite an emotionally based card, for sometimes it can appear to denote resolution of long term problems, the end of damaging relationships, and the overall triumph of the being in life. Look for cards such as the 6 of Cups or Wands again, or the 9 or 10 of Cups (the 9 would be particularly auspicious, since it is the Wish card, and indicates that what you dream with all your heart will come true)

Since there is an immense amount of driving energy in the Chariot, it is important to pay attention to cards which might block that flow of energy – 7 of Cups, 5 or 10 of Wands, and 7 or 8 of Swords would all indicate stagnation or blocking of intent. Here, look carefully to see whether you feel the obstacles are coming from your querent or from some other source. Court cards may show, as could the archetypal Majors – Magician through Empress – to denote a person getting in the way. If you feel negativity is coming from your querent look for cards which indicate what they need to do – 8 of Wands would mean communicating clearly, whilst the 7 of Wands or Lust might instruct them to keep going regardless of what they feel stands in their path. The 7 of Swords might show a lack of self-belief, as could the 5 of Cups.

The attention-to-detail aspect is emphasised even more if the Chariot comes up with the 3 of Disks or the Universe – each of these cards has a lot to say about natural order, and about how one thing leads to another. With Aces, the Chariot will show the start of the next stage of the journey – look to the Suit of the Ace to tell you where efforts should be directed.

ADJUSTMENT

Adjustment was formerly known as Justice, and still carries many of the interpretations from that form. However the modern version of the card has been extended to include higher matters of balance and equilibrium, which were somewhat missing from the traditional card. I will try to cover both versions here. Even if you use a deck in which this card is called Justice, it's worth building the more extended meanings into your interpretation of it.

The legal and formal aspects of this card are strongly emphasised when it comes up with Wands, especially if the Universe also appears. With the 6 of Wands you would predict success in a legal matter. With the 10, delays are inevitable, and it is possible that obstacles will cause problems. With the 2 or the 3, justice will be done. With the 4, a satisfactory, though not necessarily perfect, solution will occur.

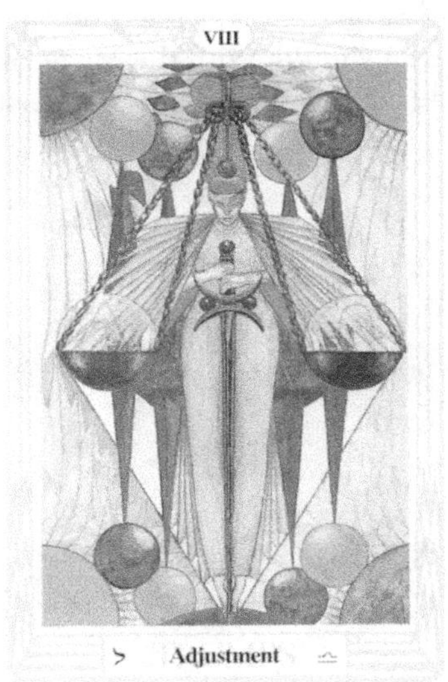

Thoth Tarot

If Adjustment appears with Swords, you will often be examining unstable and possibly immoral behaviour. With the 10, Adjustment indicates that if the querent does not stabilise swiftly, damage will quite probably be done to the overall environment. With the 8, there's a possibility that your querent is subject to the interference of another person, which needs to be stopped. With the 9, especially if the Devil or Death appears, there is a potential for real disturbance and danger. However, with the 2 or the 4 of Swords, so long as the querent remains centred, problems will eventually resolve.

Adjustment with other balance cards indicates a strong need for calm deliberation, and attention to detail. If other cards indicate disruption, the querent can be reassured that they can master the situation they find themselves in, so long as they look to their inner selves for strength, and for answers.

Hard Cups, like the 5 or 8, are softened by Adjustment, once again assuring the querent that they have what they need to find their way through whatever currently faces them.

With cards like Art and Lust, Adjustment becomes a celebration of life itself. The querent is living from the very heart of themselves, and life is unfolding as it should. With the Magician, we are viewing an individual who is creating life in the pattern they have visualised.

THE HERMIT

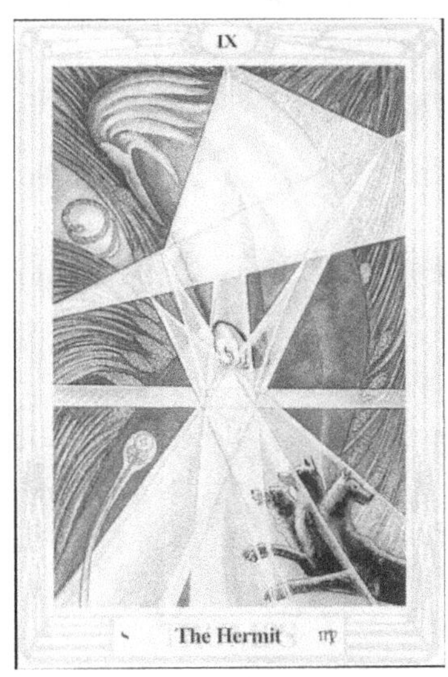

Thoth Deck

The Hermit can be a confusing card when it comes up in a reading – this is because its mundane interpretation is so far removed from its spiritual application. We have to rely on our own intuition, and the cards which surround it, to get to grips with the level at which we should be reading – as well, of course, as considering the nature of the question being posed.

Cards which would show that a spiritual interpretation should be applied are the High Priestess, Hierophant, Art, the Star, high Cups or the Ace, 6 or 8 of Wands. Fundamentally the Hermit means that we must apply ourselves to our own spiritual growth, and that, most often, the answers we require already exist within us. The Priestess or the Star particularly would indicate that this information can be released by meditation. Art would suggest that time needs to elapse whilst we make the necessary steps toward growth. The Wands would imply that action is required, either to help us release the info we need, or to implement realisations recently made.

When the Hermit appears in a more mundane context, potential interpretations change quite a bit. He can either indicate a need to retreat from a situation, event or person, or that we have already withdrawn to a dangerous extent and are now isolating ourselves.

The need to retreat would probably be accompanied by cards like the Moon, the 7, 8 or 9 of Swords, the Devil, the 5 of Cups, or the Tower. Here we are in a hazardous situation and retreat is the safest form of protection. Expect to also see cards following the Hermit to show what will happen when your querent does retreat. The 2 or 4 of Swords, or the 2 or 3 of Wands would indicate good results.

But how about when a person has already backed off defensively to an extent where they are becoming estranged from reality? Here, look for the 10 of Swords, the Death card, the 8 of Cups, the 3 or 5 of Swords. Also expect to see encouraging cards about what will happen if they face their fears and confront their personal demons. Cards like the 8 or 9 of Wands would be good, or perhaps the 9 of Cups.

FORTUNE

This is a lovely card, bringing in bright opportunities, lots of hope and unexpected turns of fate which can sometimes affect the rest of your life. As with most Major Arcana cards it is important to try to pin down the level at which the card is working when it appears in a reading. Fortune will rarely come up in a spiritual sense except to mark the final attainment of goals as a result of sheer hard work – so when the card indicates unexpected events we can rule out the higher areas of life.

However it could show that material matters are going very well, either as a relatively transient effect (you get the job or pass the exams) or on a longer term level (a run of negativity comes to an end, bringing in brighter, more optimistic times)

Thoth Tarot

Which nuance you are observing can be established by checking the cards around it – if you see cards like the Ace or 2 of Disks, the 6 of Disks, or the 9, chances are you are looking at a beneficial shift in the material area.

The Ace of Wands, with the 3 of Disks, 7 or 8 of Wands, 9 of Cups or Wands, or the 10 of Cups might indicate extremely positive progress in a heartfelt project. Fortune following big change cards like Death or the Tower would show sweeping and disruptive changes that lead to better times. Court cards supported by Fortune would suggest that the person indicated is moving into a very successful period.

Fortune with Death and the Ace or 10 of Disks often indicates an inheritance (though with little concomitant grief) or other dramatic change in financial circumstances. This combination would be unlikely to represent salary growth though – look rather for the 9 or 10 of Disks to support this interpretation. The 3 of Disks can also sometimes predict unexpected money coming in.

The very most auspicious reading will contain Fortune and the Star – the closer together the better, so long as neither of them appears in a 'past' position. The Star is THE card for incoming, Universe-blessed opportunities, and Fortune serves to reinforce the external nature of events. Look also for cards which indicate the direction the good fortune will come from, and how the querent should be using the opportunities on offer.

LUST

Thoth Tarot

This is a bright, high energy card, bringing in enthusiasm and dynamism. These qualities are heightened if it accompanies the Emperor, or the Ace of Wands in a reading. Each of these suggests a force of will applied with precision and a sense of fascination which compels success in endeavours. When this combination also presents the Magus, then we are looking at a startling and powerful period in the querent's experience.

If Lust appears with the Sun, then the emphasis shifts toward the healing properties of each card. Look for other indications to pin down where healing will take place. Cups or high Swords would imply stormy relationships and emotional situations. Disks could show physical healing of ailments, or a stabilisation in the family environment.

One component of this card which is very important is the question of right attention. Read over the section in the "Working With" area to remind yourself of this concept. When Lust appears with Art the need for Right Attention is paramount – life is talking to you. You need to give yourself time to listen.

Lust with the Devil can look like a rather dangerous pairing until you remember the aspect of the Devil which deals with throwing off inhibitions and restrictions. However it is as well, if you find this combination, to keep an eye open for the 7 of Cups – that group could suggest overwhelming temptation to break the rules in the heat of the moment.

Lust appearing with most Wands will be strengthened in a reading, whereas if there are a lot of Cups in a reading with Lust, then the Major could lend a certain additional turbulence to events.

And there is one particular situation in which Lust becomes an unhelpful – even quite ugly - card. When you are reading low self-esteem, with cards like 7, 9 or 10 of Swords, and when there is clearly a great deal of stress surrounding your querent, Lust takes up a role rather like a steam vent – everything builds up to bursting point, then the Lust energy blasts away. In this circumstance there will often be rows and discord, indicated by cards like 5 of Wands or the Tower.

THE HANGED MAN

There are two separate aspects of the Hanged Man that need to be considered when interpreting his appearance in a reading. First and foremost, you need to identify whether he represents a problem – perhaps with moving forward, or taking decisive action; or whether he represents a spiritually revealing period in which the querent will make new breakthroughs.

Thoth Tarot

If his appearance indicates the former condition, expect to find other 'blockage' cards appearing nearby. The 10 of Wands, or the 5 or 8 of Cups would indicate this, as would the 7 of Swords. With these cards present, the Hanged Man would very likely be pointing to personal challenges which are not being well met, or showing that energies are blocked, rather than free- flowing. Look for cards that represent courses of action to alleviate the problem. Bear in mind that the Hanged Man can indicate inertia, laziness, and lack of dynamism. Cards such as the 8 of Disks, the 7 of Wands or the 3 of Disks would show that steady effort was required to effect change.

If, on the other hand, the appearance of the Hanged Man marked a period of spiritual growth, you would expect to see Art (Temperance), the Hermit, the Star, the Sun or the Moon present. You might also find a large number of good Swords here. Do not be perturbed if you see the Tower in an instructional position – there can often be a pause immediately preceding breakthrough, and the growth itself can sometimes cause disruption or upheaval for a time. In this case, look for cards which indicate a return to balance like Adjustment, Art or Lust.

There is one other situation in which the Hanged Man will sometimes occur in a reading. You will remember that this card can indicate a necessity to surrender control, and allow events to follow a natural course. Here you might find Death up with the Hanged Man – or challenging cards like the 9 or 10 of Swords. One particular combination to keep your eyes open for is where this card is accompanied either by the 8 of Swords (let things develop on their own for a little while) or the 10 of Cups (all things have their rightful moment in time and will best transpire when that time arrives).

Sometimes we have no choice but to simply sit back and accept. The Hanged Man is probably the primary card in the deck to indicate that outside events must be allowed to play out their role without interference.

DEATH

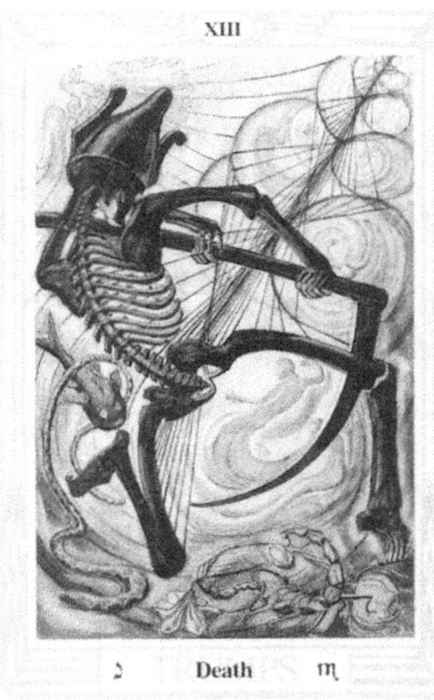

Thoth Tarot

As we know, this card indicates sweeping changes. These will often lead to renewal and regrowth after out-dated issues, situations or thoughts have been cleared out of the querent's path. But one thing that can cause problems for the reader is defining exactly what kind of change is going to happen. Also, we must face the fact that sometimes the card means exactly what it says – somebody in the querent's immediate vicinity is going to die. We have to have a strategy for coping with this particular possibility. And we need to bear in mind that Death usually brings with it disruptive or disturbing influences, and often a sense of shock, since events happen without warning.

Let's take a look at some card combinations. The worst possible combinations would be the Death card coming up with the Tower and high Swords. The appearance of the 3 of Swords here would almost certainly indicate that an actual death will take place. The high Swords could indicate a violent death.

Death with the Hanged Man, invert Sun (if you use reversals), invert Ace of Wands, the 10 of Wands, or the 7 of Swords may indicate death after a long illness. The card appearing with the Aeon (Judgement), the Universe, the 4 of Wands or the 2 of Swords could indicate the type of death which is peaceful, and a happy release.

Death followed by any Ace will generally mean a traumatic change in the area covered by the Ace – for instance, Death followed by the 5 or 7 of Disks and the Ace of Disks might indicate a sudden end of employment, followed by worry, but where the querent quickly gets another position.

Death with (say) the 5, 7 or 8 of Swords, or the 5 or 7 of Cups would tend to suggest the sudden and unexpected end of a romantic or other close relationship. If you saw the Universe later in the reading, or the 4 of Wands this would indicate that the relationship will end in divorce. If, on the other hand, Death were followed by the 2 or 3 of Cups there's a fair chance of reconciliation – though this would need to be supported later by stable cards like the 9 or 10 of Cups or the Lovers.

I have to say that, when giving advanced reading techniques like these, because of the sheer complexity of the Tarot as a reading tool, you as the reader must always rely firmly on your own intuition. There are so many variants of interpretation in any reading that whilst I can give you pointers to look for... in the end I could write two or three hundred of these combinations before I even begin to fully cover a given card.

ART

Some people find Art (or Temperance) a little tricky to interpret at times. I think this stems from the influences created by the multiplicity of underlying meanings – those referring to the Great Magickal Art, matters more connected to how we relate, day-to-day to life, the ways in which we relate to events which occur and which seem at variance with what we have Willed for ourselves.

Thoth Tarot

Every now and again this card will burst forth into a reading with a resounding 'bang'. At those times, it may well be accompanied by spiritual cards like the Priestess, the Star or, perhaps, a Cup Court. This is when we need to consider the massive force for spiritual transformation that comes with Art. Such periods can be bumpy and demanding – so don't be surprised to see cards like the Tower, Death, or high Swords showing up too.

However, much more often, when Art appears, it is pointing to the necessity to re-centre ourselves. It will often come up during troublesome periods, marked by some of the more difficult cards in the deck. Expect to see the 5, 7 or 8 of

Cups, or 5, 8, 9 or 10 of Swords. We encounter adversity and are counselled to employ patience, and objectivity.

In this case, Art is reminding us of our need to make sure we maintain an overview of life in order to keep perspective. Perhaps one area of life threatens to overwhelm us, and we are focussing all our attention on that, instead of recognising that no one area of life can be allowed to dominate. It is a very rare event where literally every single area of life "betrays" us at any one time. This imbalance arises often where there is money pressure – we feel threatened by our financial situation, shown by 2 or 5 of Disks say – and we fail to pay attention to our satisfying, happy relationships – when the 4, 5 or 8 of Cups will arise, and so on...

When this card appears with cards like Adjustment (Justice), the Universe and the Ace of Swords, it can refer to legal dealings and their eventual satisfactory outcome. With cards like Fortune or the Sun, it often marks achievement or recovery.

THE DEVIL

Thoth Tarot

This is often a card which challenges readers, leading to the occasional misplaced interpretation. At its very worst, it is, of course, an ugly influence to appear in a reading. But on many occasions it has a far less daunting and unpleasant effect than might be imagined in the first instance.

On the principle of getting the worst aspect of the card out of the way first, let us examine the dark side of the Devil. If it appears with cards like the 9 or 10 of Swords, then there is a strong possibility that we are observing mindless destruction and cruelty, either by or at the querent.

Here it would be important to look for Court cards to indicate whether another individual is involved. The 8 of Swords would be another indicator of external pressure. But remember, we can be our own worst enemies, and can do more damage to ourselves than can anybody else. If no cards appear to indicate external others, then the pain and suffering caused are of our own making.

The 7 or 8 of Cups could also emphasise that external pressures are having influence. These would usually be romantic attachments of one sort or another. The 4 of Cups (especially with the Moon) would show that we have built up illusions around a given situation which bear little relation with reality.

The Devil with the 10 of Wands would indicate that we are blocked in important areas of life leading to frustration and confusion. This card with the 8 of Swords would suggest that a difficult situation needs to be left alone for a time, in order that it can begin to unravel naturally. With Death, this card would show that we are having problems coming to terms with a situation we do not like, that has changed our expectations of life. With the 5 of Wands, we are suffering as a result of an avoidable conflict, and possibly maintaining hostilities long after they serve any useful purpose.

The Devil with the Emperor assumes a much lighter view of the card. Now we are examining our base instincts and responses. Sexuality and the male drive comes to the fore here. Look for cards like Lust, the 6 of Cups and the 2 of Swords to indicate natural and comfortable expression of basic drives and needs. More negative cards would be the 7 of Swords, the 10 of Wands or the 7 of Cups. Each of these would represent repressive attitudes toward natural activities.

With Lust alone the Devil becomes a joyous and celebrational card where love of life is expressed freely and without fear. Art (Temperance) would be another supportive card here, implying that the free flow of sexual will allows for a true engagement with life.

It is very important to bear in mind that the Devil is a card which engages primarily with our most basic urges. And it is the primal factor in our race which brings out both the very best and the very worst in us.

THE TOWER

This card tends to be viewed with a certain reserve when it turns up in a reading – it can indicate unpleasantness and disruption. However it is important to remember that, by and large, the events indicated by this card are usually important steps forward along the life path, and any resistance to them will gradually build up until it breaks through willy-nilly into life.

To ascertain whether your querent is making problems for themselves by resisting change, look for cards like the 7 of Swords, the 10 of Wands, or the 7 or 8 of Cups. Any of these would suggest that the querent is getting in their own way, either with faulty belief systems or with woolly headed thinking.

Thoth Tarot

If the Tower appears after the Death card in a reading, changes will already have begun and it is important to guide the querent toward acceptance. If you also see the 9 or 10 of Swords, it is likely that that the situation is being made considerably worse by their resistance. In this case you would need to guide them toward opening their minds so that change causes the least amount of difficulty.

If the Tower comes up with the Fool then you can confidently advise that your querent should be prepared to take some risks. Look out for cards like the Star, Fortune, the 6 of Wands or the 6 of Disks to indicate a satisfactory and rewarding outcome.

With the 7 of Wands, you would advise that whilst the actions required may demand courage, they will pay off in the end. With Aces, the Tower indicates new avenues of exploration.

When the Tower appears with the Star, the High Priestess or the Hierophant you are probably looking at major leaps of spiritual faith, probably precipitous though beneficial. Look also here for cards like the Chariot or the Ace of Cups to indicate how upcoming changes will affect the querent.

However when the Tower appears either with the Devil or with the 7 of Cups you need to issue warnings to your querent that they are liable to take a wrong turn along the way, opting for base or instinctual choices which will come into conflict with their moral convictions. If you see the 5 of Cups here too then such actions will lead to severe disappointment and shame.

THE STAR

Thoth Tarot

This is such a bountiful and happy card that it always has a great impact on any reading in which it appears. Keep an eye out for one particularly show-stopping combination – when the Star appears with Fortune in a reading, it will mark a really outstanding fortuitous time during which any and all opportunities should be maximised.

The Star can come up to indicate good progress in any area at all. Firstly, you can take an overview of the reading to try to pin down the area of influence. Lots of Cups and Major Arcana cards could point to spiritual matters – even more likely if the Priestess, Magician or Hierophant appear.

Wands and Disks would point at career matters and financial areas. Disks alone would show positive movement in the material side of life. Just Wands would cover any projects and ambitions your querent holds dear. Swords and the Star are very likely to indicate conflict and dispute being resolved. A good spread across all suits would mark one of those remarkable periods where life goes right on all fronts.

Once you have determined which area of life the Star is influencing, you can centre down on the actual cards that turn up in the reading. Remember the effect of the Star is to clarify and positively progress any situation at all, no matter how troublesome.

If this card appears with Aces then new projects should be launched as soon as possible. However if the Chariot also appears, advise your querent not to rush things in their eagerness to get going.

Look for 6s – these indicate the success and fulfilment that will come from the launch of the project – Disks point to financial prosperity, Wands overall success and satisfaction perhaps after struggle, Swords in this context would tend to relate to peace of mind and rest from conflict with the Star, and Cups could indicate happy relationships, or the success of heartfelt projects.

5s might indicate a certain amount of obstruction and difficulty, but the Star always gives the querent the power to deal with any such problems. Watch for cards which show you how to guide and advise the querent, such as the 8 of Wands (the querent needs to communicate to overcome the issue), the 8 of Swords (they should give it a little time), or the 8 of Disks (a warning to proceed with caution and confidence).

If the Universe (World) or Adjustment (Justice) comes up, advise your querent to pay particular attention to the official and legal details surrounding the project or opportunity in question.

THE MOON

This is a complex card to interpret, and so its effect is sometimes minimised. Readers will often use the more obvious aspects of deceit and illusion for interpretation when it appears. In fact, the Moon in a reading can indicate major spiritual growth and huge leaps of realisation. It is important to consider surrounding cards in order to work out which aspects of this card are applicable at the time.

With the 5 or 7 of Cups, the Devil, or the Page of Swords, there is a fair chance that deceit and dishonesty are indeed having influence. The Page, particularly, can point to a specific person who is deliberately giving a false impression. The Tower can indicate a shocking and uncomfortable period where deceit and dishonesty is finally exposed – this may be accompanied by harsh Cups or high Swords to denote the distress felt by the person deceived.

Thoth Tarot

But with the Chariot, Death or the High Priestess we are more likely to be entering the realm of spiritual growth. Death especially indicates the possibility of some major breakthrough, or initiation. Look here also for cards like the Hierophant, or the Hermit to show the possibility of new teachers emerging to guide the querent along their path.

With cards like the 8 of Cups, or the 9 or 10 of Swords, there is a possibility that the illusory qualities of the Moon are coming to the fore. This might be underlined if the Magician is also present – he is a master of making things appear to be what he wants them to be.

When the Moon appears followed immediately or quickly by the Sun in a reading, you may well be encountering the cyclic changes of life's pattern – day and night, season on season. Look also for the Wheel of Fortune, or the Universe to reinforce this interpretation.

THE SUN

Thoth Tarot

The Sun is a warm and happy card, signifying healing, fresh reserves of energy and the realisation of ambitions and hopes. It is especially strengthened when it appears with Lust, and with the Ace of Wands. This is because these cards are all about inrushes of positive energy.

When it follows difficult cards like the 3 or 7 of Swords, it will often mark a period where an individual returns to full good health after sickness. Look also for cards like Art, the 4 of Wands or the Universe. These would show that recovery is total, and an awkward phase in life has come to an end.

When the Sun comes up with the Star, we can expect to find our querent moving into a remarkably fortunate and beneficial period. This will often be marked by strong cards for change as well, like Death, the Tower or the 2 of Disks.

With Fortune, the Sun tends to focus most strongly on projects already in hand, indicating that good progress will be made, and that the querent can expect success and satisfaction. Followed by cards like the 6 of Wands, or Disks, this effect is further strengthened.

When the Sun directly follows the Moon in a reading you will see your querent moving into less stormy waters – and possibly having certain areas clarified which have, before, been clouded or confused. This combination can indicate that deliberate deceptions are being revealed – though this can be uncomfortable for the querent, it usually means that obstacles can be removed, and that life can proceed more normally, or fairly. Look for cards like Adjustment, or the Universe to confirm this interpretation.

The Sun immediately preceding the Aeon shows that your querent is moving through a period of great spiritual change. They will develop a stronger ability to reach for the overview, and to get the whole picture. Things will fall into place which have hitherto been mystified.

THE AEON

This card is heavily reliant for accurate interpretation on the cards around it. It can indicate something relatively simple like the requirement for a clear-cut decision about something. In this case it will be accompanied by cards like the Ace or 2 of Swords, both underlining the need for decisive action. If there has previously been confusion or delay, you may see cards like the 3, 7 or 8 of Swords, or the 7 of Cups.

However, the Aeon can also represent important spiritual breakthroughs, and here will be accompanied by 'teaching' cards like the High Priestess or the Hierophant. Keep an eye open for the Star here, because this would indicate a really significant step forward.

Thoth Tarot

With the advent of new style decks, one particular function of the Aeon has become a little clouded – that is, in the area of legal and official decisions and verdicts. You will sometimes see this card accompanied by Adjustment (Justice) and in these cases you are almost certainly looking at an issue of this type. You may also find the Ace of Swords here again. Keep an eye open for subsequent indications about how things will go from the perspective of the querent. Cards like the 7 of Disks or Cups will probably indicate that the final decision will not be favourable. The Sun, the Ace of Wands, the 2 of Swords, the Chariot, or Fortune would all indicate a good outcome. If the Universe was showing, you would say that the end result would be fair – if not entirely satisfactory.

The Aeon will also sometimes come up to show a period of self-realisation and fresh inner knowledge. Expect to see cards like the Queen of Swords, the Hermit, the Hanged Man, or the 8 of Disks to indicate growth and understanding. There may be some discomfort showing during a period like this – the development of personal understanding can be a gritty experience. If you see cards like the 7 or 8 of Swords, there will be personal doubt. The 10 of Wands or Swords would imply that your querent is feeling too overwhelmed and negative to work through this process efficiently.

THE UNIVERSE

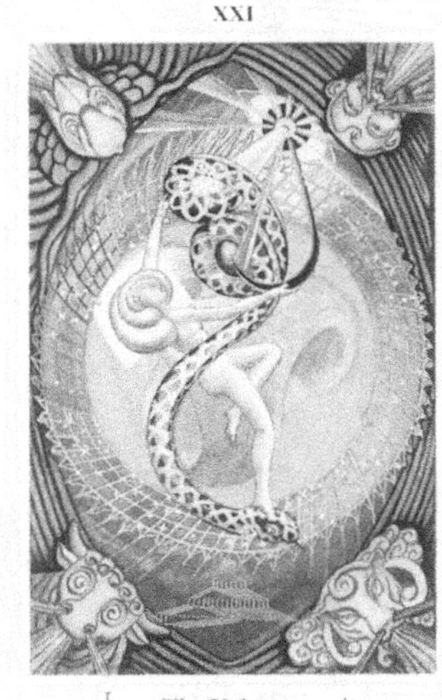

ħ   The Universe   ☽

Thoth Tarot

This card indicates reaching a stage of completion. Often matters in the querent's life are coming to a point of change. Certain things will end, and other opportunities and directions will emerge. The way a person approaches such periods of change can have a strong effect on how the individual is feeling, and it is worth keeping an eye open for any cards which reveal this. If a querent is fearful of, or dreading change, their fears will tend to darken how you see the reality of forward movement.

With the 4 of Wands, this card will often show the formal end or point of closure in a matter that probably had some personal investment for your querent. There will frequently be cards indicating emotional responses here, which need to be taken into account to give best guidance.

If the Universe appears with Adjustment or Justice, there are quite possibly legal dealings afoot. This may also be true if the Aeon (Judgement) arises. The Hierophant or the Emperor here might denote people able to make judgements which affect the querent. Look for cards which indicate the eventual outcome – 6 of Wands, 6 of Disks, or the Sun would all be confirmations of a good outcome.

In more mundane readings, the Universe tends to come up most often to mark external events and their effects upon your querent. It is rarely, of itself, a particularly spiritual card. However on those remarkable occasions when a person reaches revelation which leads to life change, then the Universe can appear to indicate a breakthrough into new areas, and will then often be accompanied by cards like the Star, the High Priestess or the Hierophant.

WANDS

ACE OF WANDS

As you know, this is a high energy card which often comes up to show the beginning of new projects. At its most influential level, it also marks the beginning of new life. Therefore it can signify pregnancy, and it can also indicate a complete turning point for an individual, during which period they change most of the familiar features of their lives and select a completely new direction.

It is not unusual for this card to appear with Major Arcana cards – this is because its energy is so powerful and all-encompassing. With Death, the Tower, or the 10 of Swords, it can indicate that shocking, unexpected events have taken place which precipitated change. Look for following cards indicating how things will

Ace of Wands

Thoth Tarot

turn out. The 9 or 10 of Cups would suggest that changes lead to emotional contentment and ease; the 9 or 10 of Disks would suggest improvement in material, family or financial areas; and the 6, 8 or 9 of Wands would show success and good progress.

If you feel the card represents pregnancy (keep an eye open for the Ace, Queen or Princess of Cups, or the Princess of Disks) then look out for cards like the Empress, the Sun and the Star to show good health and a happy result.

If this Ace appears with Lust (Strength) then the indication of huge power is strongly amplified, since they are both very high powered cards. Look for cards like the 6 of Disks or Wands to show positive movement. Regard the 3 or 4 of Disks as a warning to contain and direct the available energy. The 10 of Cups might indicate slight delays, then excellent realisation of hopes. The 7 of Swords might show a tendency not to use energy efficiently, as might the 7 of Cups. When the Ace of Wands appears with the Sun or the Star, you are examining a very auspicious time in your querent's life.

TWO OF WANDS

Dominion

Thoth Tarot

The Lord of Dominion is a powerful card, which usually recognises effort toward, and struggle for, autonomy. When it follows the Ace of Wands, it will generally indicate that a particular project is well-equipped to succeed, so then you would be looking for cards such as the 6 of Disks or Wands to suggest eventual good outcomes.

When the 2 of Wands appears with either the Magician or the 9 of Cups (the wish card) you are examining a particularly auspicious period where the querent would be hard pushed to put a foot wrong. If the Star also appears, this will generally be a time when all activities are likely to succeed. Advise the querent to take advantage of everything that comes their way.

Sometimes this 2 will emerge to indicate a successful struggle with matters like low self-esteem. In this case, look for the 7 of Swords or the 7 of Disks to give you some idea about whether troubles have been emotionally or materially based. Cards such as the 4 of Wands or the Universe would indicate that recovery will be complete and permanent.

The 2 of Wands is strengthened when it appears with cards like the Emperor – here you are most likely examining a man in a position of great power and influence. It is important to look at the cards surrounding this combination to ascertain whether this influence will be beneficial or damaging for the querent. Cards such as the Tower, high Swords, or 2 of Disks may not bode too well.

When you see the Lord of Dominion coming up in a largely emotionally based reading, the chances are the querent is reclaiming their own life and direction after a period of surrender to some-one or something else. With difficult emotional cards, they may be emerging from a damaging relationship. With the Empress, they may be facing the period where a woman emerges from the responsibilities of motherhood, for example.

THREE OF WANDS

The 3 of Wands, Lord of Virtue, is unique in this active and dynamic suit because it holds a degree of inner contemplation and calmness. Having achieved a given set of goals in our journey on life's path, we can see ourselves at rest – in repose. We can see to the far horizon, but as yet we are not galvanised to strive toward it.

For this reason this can be a remarkably welcome card when it appears in readings that indicate a good deal of earlier discontent or pain. After the turbulence of the 8, 9, or 10 of Swords, the upheaval of Death or the Tower, the sadness of the 3 of Swords or the 5 of Cups, we find ourselves reaching safe harbour when the 3 of Wands appears. Look for cards further on in the reading to show how long the period of recovery is liable to last, and also for indications as to where our thoughts will eventually settle when considering our future.

Thoth Tarot

Disks might indicate us throwing ourselves into our work, whereas Aces might imply that when we emerge from our convalescence we will be headed for pastures new. The 2 of Wands would show that we have achieved new levels of mastery as a result of our recovery time, whereas Cups like the 3 or the 6 might suggest we will enthusiastically start or extend some creative pursuits to begin to build a new direction.

After any period of high activity, this card will indicate a pause – and perhaps a time for consolidation and regrouping. Again, the cards which follow will give us clues about the direction we shall choose for our next endeavour. When this 3 appears with Art, the period may be enforced from outside, life itself demanding that we take time to count our blessings.

Because the Lord of Virtue has a great deal to tell us about returning to the centre of our being, it is especially reinforced by cards like the Hermit, which will warn us to rely purely upon ourselves during this time. The appearance of cards like the High Priestess or the Hierophant may point to the influence of external factors, or teachers, guiding us forward.

With the Wheel of Fortune, or the Star, though we appear to be at rest, we need to remain alert to the possibility of new opportunities coming our way. With the Emperor, we are looking at the pause before dynamic effort toward our goals. This can also be true if you see the Princess of Disks, or the Chariot – both cards which prepare us for the next stage in our journey.

The Hanged Man might imply that there is a temptation to remain too long in a comfortable position, especially if coupled with the 4 of Disks – which can indicate us settling for the status quo, and being unwilling to take risks.

FOUR OF WANDS

Completion

Thoth Tarot

The unquenchable exuberance of Wands solidifies here into achievement and celebration. The Lord of Completion marks the end of a phase, which allows new horizons to open out before the querent. There is usually a sense of satisfaction and fulfilment when this card appears.

As previously mentioned, this 4 has much in common with the Universe – both marking the end of cycles in life. Whereas the Universe will normally point to big life changes, the Lord of Completion will come up to indicate the smaller, yet still significant, shifts along the path. With the 6 of Disks, a business project will come to a successful and satisfactory conclusion. With the 6 of Swords we may be looking at a more spiritually oriented group of events. With the 6 of Wands, breakthrough is achieved after struggle.

If this 4 appears with the Tower, we are probably examining a person who is fighting their way out of a restrictive and difficult period in life. This may also be true if the Lord of Completion turns up with the Devil in close proximity. Look, in this circumstance, for recovery cards to best direct your querent. You will often find the 2 of Swords up during a time like this, indicating the necessity to make important decisions, and the inner peace thus derived.

When this card appears with Adjustment (Justice) we may be looking at the satisfactory completion of some sort of formal documentation, or legal matter. With the 8 of Disks it is possible that a period of study has been completed successfully.

This card rarely comes up with Aces – they indicate starts, and this card shows closure. Therefore if you do get the Lord of Completion with an Ace, it may emphasise the necessity of seeing a course of action through to its final end, regardless of the consequences.

FIVE OF WANDS

As with most cards, the effects of the Lord of Strife must be seen as a sliding scale. At the most transient level this card can indicate momentary conflict – with oneself or with others. Look for Courts to indicate whether there is a row brewing with somebody else. Look also for cards like the 7 of Swords, or the 8 of Cups, to indicate that trouble has been brewing for a while. This would suggest there are unresolved problems which need to be sorted out.

Thoth Tarot

If no Courts show, then the problem is within the querent – they have issues which have strong influence but which they have difficulty in resolving. In either case, expect to find cards indicating the best method of dealing with the current strife. The Ace of Swords, or the Aeon (Judgement) would suggest a decision is needed; if either of these was followed by the 2 of Swords, then finally taking a firm decision will bring peace of mind.

If the 5 of Wands comes up with harder cards like the 9 or 10 of Swords, you must view the situation more seriously. Again, look for Courts in order to work out whether there are outside influences at work. And remember also to look at whether it is your querent causing the difficulty, rather than having the difficulty put in their path. If your querent shows as the Knight or Queen of Swords, there's a possibility s/he has greater responsibility. Look also for cards like the Devil, 5 of Cups, 7 of Cups – these cards would indicate an unhealthy depth of feeling which could lead to rash actions.

In these cases, look for resolution cards, and don't forget that some situations are dealt with best by simply walking away from them. The 8 of Cups or 10 of Wands might indicate this is the safest course of action.

SIX OF WANDS

Victory

Thoth Tarot

It is important to remember that the Lord of Victory, whilst a triumphant card, does not usually come into play without a struggle beforehand. So do not be surprised to see the 6 of Wands appear following challenging or difficult periods. Here, we examine the moment of break-through – often when we had given up hope of achieving what we need. For this reason, the Tower or the Devil can frequently be close companions to this card. They may indicate the loosening of restrictions, or breakthrough into new areas.

The 4 of Wands and the Universe often also come up with the Lord of Victory, for this card will indicate long- fought and hard-won battles, which bring a given area of importance to completion. The Chariot is another card which can regularly appear with this one, indicating that, though the battle is won, the war is not necessarily yet over. The 4 of Swords would contribute to this effect.

The Fool is another favourite card to turn up with the Lord of Victory –

frequently the conclusion of one phase will lead to the beginning of another, and that new course of action may require risks and open-heartedness.

Look for several of a suit to indicate which area of life might be affected. Disks would mean general mundane matters – domestic issues, or the work environment. Cups (and sometimes Swords) could point us toward the more emotional and turbulent of our relationships. It is also true that Swords could indicate legal matters. Wands would generally indicate matters of Will, ambition and heartfelt projects.

Hard won victories can sometimes lead us to be less than moral when dealing with our opponents – watch out for cards following this one that suggest that victory is not truly graciously accepted. The 8 or 9 of Swords might suggest a tendency toward unkindness by, or toward, your querent.

If this card is followed by the 7 of Wands or Swords, an interesting effect is liable to take place – the initial conflict has absorbed so much energy that it has had a negative effect upon the querent. Once success is achieved, they will find themselves with new and fresh reserves of strength. This interpretation could easily be confirmed by cards like the Ace of Wands, or Lust (Strength). Such changes need to be carefully directed in order to get the best out of any given situation with which the querent engages.

SEVEN OF WANDS

We have already discussed how closely connected the Lord of Valour is with acts of courage. When it appears in a reading, you will always be examining actions or undertakings about which there is a certain amount of anxiety and fear. Your querent will probably have doubts about their ability to successfully follow through effectively.

Look for cards which indicate that they will be successful in their endeavours in order to reassure them. The Sun, the Chariot, or the Ace, 4 or 8 of Wands would all be good indicators that risks are worth taking. With the Fool, action is greatly encouraged too.

Thoth Tarot

Inertia is the enemy of the 7 of Wands so look for cards which may indicate blockages, like the 5 or 10 of Wands, or the 7 of Swords, to try to identify and eliminate these.

The 7 of Cups would tell you that courage is required in an emotional context, so look also for cards that show who else is involved and how. You might find Court cards here for the people or person to whom courage must be shown. Cards like the Lovers would mark the primary relationship in somebody's life.

Sometimes the Lord of Valour will come up to indicate the querent working up the determination and courage to move away from unhealthy situations and contacts. Then you might find the Tower is also present to indicate whether, if they take no actions themselves, your querent will have matters forced upon them. Death would indicate a definite and conclusive break. But if you also saw the Hanged Man then perhaps the querent is delaying necessary action.

EIGHT OF WANDS

Swiftness

Thoth Tarot

The Lord of Swiftness is a card which marks rapid changes, swift thinking and a sudden and unexpected approach to seemingly impossible goals. When it appears with the Star, the Priestess or the Hierophant it can indicate massive expansion spiritually.

If it appears with Aces it indicates the beginning of some new project – or even a relationship with the Ace of Cups. Keep an eye open here for warning cards, because an Ace energy coupled with the 8 of Wands can sometimes lead to rashness. The Tower would be a powerful warning, whereas cards like the 7 of Cups would indicate more forethought is required.

When the Lord of Swiftness appears with the Hanged Man, intractable problems can be resolved. Look for cards such as the 4 of Wands or the Sun to indicate satisfactory resolution.

If this card appears with the Death card pay attention to which order the cards are dealt. With Death first a sudden unpredictable event has occurred which demands rapid thinking and the ability to follow through swiftly. If the 8 appears first, sudden brainwaves lead to enormous change.

With the Aeon, your querent is stood on a threshold, making important decisions which may well be life-altering. New methods of approaching decisions need to be employed in order to reach conclusion. With the Universe, conclusions are reached and implemented, and a new phase begins.

It is quite interesting to note the influence that this 8 has on the other 8s through the Suits. Even the Major 8 is fairly limiting and demanding – Adjustment requires that attitudes must be changed in order to attain balance. The 8 of Disks, Prudence, requires that care be taken during a period of development. The 8 of Cups, Indolence, shakes the querent out of their torpor. The 8 of Swords, Interference, suggest outside limitation. And then along comes the 8 of Wands like a gale-force wind to break down anything that gets in the way of resolution.

The Lord of Swiftness and the Fool might suggest new adventures which probably need a little more planning, and have a warning against swift ill-considered action. With Fortune, this card indicates a rapid and successful approach to a long-held goal. With the Hermit, this 8 becomes something of a warning card itself – don't dwell too much on the inner life, for in order to progress, inner realisation must manifest in the outside world.

NINE OF WANDS

The Lord of Strength is a welcome card to appear in a reading. It is especially emphasised if cards such as Lust (Strength) or the Sun accompany it. These are both high energy cards which accentuate the 9 of Wands' sense of vigour and dynamism.

Because this card talks of a person's inner strength, it will sometimes come up after a period of strife and tension. If you also see the 7 of Swords, then you can reassure your querent that despite any feeling to the contrary, they have the power to complete the tasks ahead of them.

If the 9 of Wands appears with cards like the 8 or 9 of Swords, it is important to stress the need for strong personal boundaries. There is a possibility here, heightened if Court cards appear, that someone will attempt to manipulate your querent.

Strength

Thoth Tarot

During periods of recovery after shock or loss, the Lord of Strength will appear to indicate the gradual process of healing that must take place. This will apply when the querent is not the person directly affected as well, indicating that they need to be prepared to lend their strength to someone close to them.

The resilience inherent to this card is often not clear to the querent. They may need to have it plainly pointed out to them. There can be instances where the querent has developed independence and strength of character through struggle to the extent that they expect the next problem, rather than simply being grateful for their own self-reliance. Be especially watchful for this if the High Priestess or the Hermit appear – either of these cards can show an unwillingness to rely on or trust others.

TEN OF WANDS

Oppression

Thoth Tarot

This card will always indicate blockages in the querent's path when it turns up in a reading. Surrounding cards will assist you in working out the nature and severity of these obstacles and difficulties. In order to determine which area of life they affect look for groups of suits to give you clues. Disks would point to work, money, family and material situation. Cups could indicate the querent's love-life, creative pursuits, or again, family. Wands would point you toward the achievement of goals, the realisation of ambition, or other operations of Will. Swords might show conflict situations, intellectual pursuits or inner turmoil. Of course, these are broad definitions, but would generally give you a starting point for locating trouble.

If this 10 stands alone, then the blockage is probably temporary and will shift over time. But some groups of cards would indicate major difficulties. With the Tower, for example, your querent is probably embarking on a course of action which life will shortly dissuade them from in an uncomfortable fashion. With Death, things can be quite serious as well – drastic change needs to take place in order for the difficulty to be resolved. With the Hanged Man, the querent is entrenched, and probably creating problems for themselves.

If Court cards come up near the 10 of Wands, your querent could be engaged in conflict with that person – look for the 5 of Wands, 7 or 8 of Swords, or 5 or 7 of Cups to define the conflict. And then look later in the reading for resolution cards – 5 of Swords or any of the aforementioned cards would indicate that there is no satisfactory resolution available, and the querent would be better off beating a hasty retreat. On the other hand cards like 2 or 3 of Cups, 2, 3 or 4 of Wands, 7 or 8 of Wands or majors such as the Star, Fortune, or Adjustment, would all suggest that problems will be overcome.

PRINCESS OF WANDS

This card brings with it a wealth of dynamic energy. When it is referring to a state of mind, the person it represents will be filled with vitality and strength. They will be eager to engage with life, and this effect is enormously strengthened when the card is accompanied by Lust (Strength). Each of these cards talks about focussed energy, willpower directed consciously in the now.

If this Princess appears with the High Priestess, or the Star, you will quite probably be looking at indications of major leaps forward in the spiritual area of life. Look also for the Hierophant to confirm this.

Princess of Wands

Thoth Tarot

Where there has been turbulence in the past, this card coupled with Art will indicate a determined effort on the part of the querent to break free of restrictions and resolve difficulties.

If it follows the 10 of Wands, or the Devil, there's a good chance that major obstacles have been overcome by personal effort. If the Tower is also present, then demanding changes will need to be made in order to establish a new direction.

The person who, at core, is Princess of Wands will be a magnetic personality, commanding attention wherever she goes. If you see her in a romantic situation, keep an eye open for warnings that her passion can sometimes burn a little too bright for her partner. Warning cards here would include the 7 or 8 of Cups, or the 8 or 9 of Swords – these latter much more serious than the former.

In a career environment, this Princess usually does well, for she has great ambition and drive. But if, in this field, she comes up with cards like the 5 or 10 of Wands, her enthusiasm could be building up problems for her. Look also for other Court cards, to indicate a possible clash of personality.

PRINCE OF WANDS

Prince of Wands

Thoth Tarot

A man represented by the Prince of Wands will usually be an energetic, interesting and friendly man, swift in his enthusiasms, generous of heart, and open to new experiences.

He works very well with cards like the Sun and the Ace of Wands, since both of these are high energy, success cards. He also benefits from turning up in a reading close to Lust (Strength), because the immediacy of Lust tempers and channels his sometimes wayward energies.

He gets along well with Cup people, other Wands and some Swords, though he can tend to be dampened by Disks. He detests dishonesty, so is very uncomfortable when cards like the Moon, the 8 of Swords and the 7 of Cups are about. But he is very happy with cards like Adjustment (Justice).

Being a crusader of sorts at heart, he works well with the Chariot, and the Ace of Swords – both of which can be warrior-type cards. He is warmed by the Empress, a little intimidated by the Emperor, and would likely run a mile from the Magician. The instability in the Magus's nature would tend to give rise to distrust.

By nature, the man represented by this card tends to be happy go lucky and open to life. So he works well with Art, the Star and Fortune. He is less comfortable with the Hanged Man, which holds back the natural flow, in his opinion. The Devil can indicate restriction on this man's high energy, but can also sometimes reveal identification with his instinctual nature – in this case, look for more cards showing whether this is a good or bad thing in the given circumstances.

His reactions to the Priestess and the Hierophant will be much shaped by the area of life in which he comes into contact with them. If they appear in a spiritual or moral context, then he will see them as teachers and guides, holding them in considerable high regard. If, however, they come up in more material areas of life – work for instance - he may have a more negative response, since they are unlikely to react particularly well to his brand of bonhomie.

His most likely chosen partners will be a Queen or Princess of Wands, or possibly a Princess of Swords. He likes the sparks that come from the active elements. He would generally find a Princess of Cups a little cloying, but the down to earth nature of the Princess of Disks may well hold strong appeal.

QUEEN OF WANDS

This is a strong and powerful card. When it appears in a reading, you will need to decide whether it indicates a view of self, or an external female. Consider first and foremost, the interpretive position in which the card comes up. Personal positions like the hopes and fears, aims or ambitions, or 'what to do' placements, would suggest the Queen represents a view of self. Positions such as past reference, external influences, 'help and hindrance' type placements are more likely to indicate an external female. The now and imminent future positions are a little more tricky – as is the final result placement.

Queen of Wands

Thoth Tarot

More information here will be revealed by the question posed; for instance, if your querent is asking about a woman of his/her acquaintance, you can proceed comfortably accepting that the Queen probably indicates that female.

Examine the cards which surround the Queen carefully - these will help you to understand her effect. With cards such as Lust or the Sun you will be looking at a strong, high energy effect, and a positive influence. With cards like the 8 of Cups or Swords, you would wonder whether perhaps her dynamic personality is causing a degree of interference.

With the Ace of Wands, the chances are that you are seeing a new project developing. Look for Disks and other Wands further along in the reading to give you some idea of how things will work out.

With demanding cards such as Death or the Tower, the Queen can indicate a very supportive influence, particularly as an outside force. Look also for cards like the Hanged Man to indicate whether your querent can simply relax and let things be organised by others.

With the Knight of Wands, you are probably examining a couple – these two Courts 'belong' together in a way that none of the others do, with the possible exception of Disks.

Remember that the Queen of Wands has a close relationship with the Empress – as archetypal mother/goddess figure. If these two cards come up close together, do also look for indications as to demands made from the family environment – Disks or 'young' Courts might show this, these being Page, Prince, or Princess.

KNIGHT OF WANDS

Knight of Wands

Thoth Tarot

When this card (or for that matter the King in a traditional deck) comes up in a reading, it will most usually represent an actual individual. He will be an energetic, dynamic man with a strong code of ethics, and a willingness to help others.

I have also mentioned, in the original commentary on this card, that this Knight can sometimes get trapped in unsatisfactory situations because of his dislike of causing pain. This may be expressed by the appearance of cards such as the 5 or 10 of Wands, the Hanged Man or the 8 of Cups nearby. There might also be cards indicating inner turmoil like the 7 of Swords, or the 5 of Cups.

This Knight will tend to do his duty – however he interprets it – sometimes to his own detriment. If he comes up with cards like the Hierophant or Adjustment (Justice) look carefully at the situation for signs that he is perhaps not following the best course of action for him. Again the 10 of Wands may occur here, or perhaps even the 10 of Swords to indicate that he is bringing about difficulty and restriction.

When this card appears with high energy cards like The Emperor, Lust (Strength), the Sun or the Ace of Wands, expect to see big shifts, fast forward movement and growth. This would most probably be in the career area – look for Disks here too. If the energy seems particularly concentrated, make sure there are no warning cards about, suggesting that he is moving too quickly for his own good.

One particular combination that would tend to lead you to interpret the Knight as representing a force rather than a person, would be if the card appeared with the 8 of Wands. The 8, as a communication card, could lead you to consider the effect of Wyrd, as discussed in our last examination of the Knight of Wands. Here you might also expect to see intuition cards like the Priestess, the Queen of Cups or the Moon.

CUPS

ACE OF CUPS

Ace of Cups

Thoth Tarot

One of the happy and joyous cards to appear in a deck, this Ace generally covers matters of love and family. It can indicate the beginning of a new, and long-lasting relationship. It can also suggest the conception of a new life (as in the beginning of pregnancy). And it can show a project so filled with heart-love as to be treasured and wonderful – often (but not always) of a creative nature.

With cards like Courts, the 2, 3, or 9 of Cups, the Lovers or the Sun, often we will be seeing the beginning of a new relationship. Look further into the reading for anything which is going to indicate the way in which the relationship is going to progress – cards like the 3 of Cups or the Lovers may imply early commitment. More difficult cards like the 8 of Swords might show unfinished business which interferes with good progress. The Universe may suggest that there are certain formal agreements which need to be made (like impending divorces for instance) before the relationship is completely free.

If this Ace turns up with the Empress, Princess of Disks or Princess of Cups, you are most likely to be looking at the conception of a baby. Look for cards after which indicate the progress of the pregnancy – Ace of Wands followed by a Page, Prince or Princess would indicate the birth itself. The 5 of Swords or Disks may indicate health problems, so look for other cards to indicate the way these are resolved – Lust, the Sun, Fortune, or the Ace of Wands would all indicate a temporary problem which is easily dealt with. The Tower, 9 or 10 Swords, the Devil could indicate more serious problems, and as we have already said, the 3 of Swords may indicate a miscarriage. Remember to be extremely careful both on interpretation and the way you convey what you are seeing.

With the Ace of Swords, the Ace of Disks can be considered to indicate the beginning of some really important and significant project, often of an artistic nature. The 8 of Disks could indicate training in, or learning about, a new skill. Other high Disks would suggest financial gain. Lust would show complete involvement and 6s would indicate great satisfaction, the level depending on the Suit. The 2 of Disks might be a sign of a necessary investment, and the Fool would indicate changing a course of action quite dramatically.

TWO OF CUPS

The Lord of Love is a beautiful card, evoking ideas of overflowing love and contentment, reconciliation and regrowth. It brings in happy, joyful feelings, a sense of renewed stability, and shows the possibility of new options opening up before the querent.

When this card follows the Ace of Cups in a reading it will indicate deepening love between two people (usually in a romantic context). When then followed by the 3 or 6 of Cups, we are almost certainly looking at a relationship which will lead to serious commitment and shared lives.

Love

Thoth Tarot

Where conflict shows in a reading between a couple, and then is followed by the 2 of Cups, there will most likely be a reconciliation. Look for strengthening cards thereafter to indicate that the union continues to thrive and develop – 6, 9, or 10 of Cups would all indicate this. However 7, 8, or 9 of Swords would imply that the compromise achieved was an uneasy one, not likely to last.

This card can also show reconciliation in deep relationships outside of the romantic arena. For instance, it may appear to indicate the healing of a family rift, or a bad argument between good friends resolved. In this case you will not pick up the 'romantic' cups as readily as cards such as the 4 or 6 of Disks, or the 4, 6 or 9 of Wands. Remember, this card deals with very important relationships in life.

Where no other person is involved and the 2 of Cups appears, it marks a significant spiritual and emotional outgrowth in the querent. They may have resolved an inner conflict, brought about a new understanding of a problem which has troubled them, or finally come to terms with something that has proved a thorn in their side for a while. Look for inward looking cards like Art, the Hermit and the Hanged Man, to strengthen this interpretation.

Sometimes, the Lord of Love will also appear to indicate the pursuit of a creative or artistic passion. Then the card notes the moment at which the querent has achieved sufficient skill to be able to make what they dream of. Look for Art, the Hierophant, the High Priestess, and the 6s to confirm this.

THREE OF CUPS

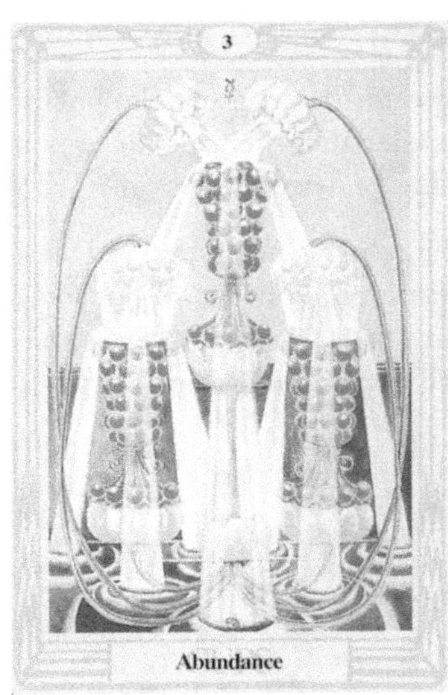

Thoth Tarot

There is something almost completely undefinable about the quality of shared emotion with those who are linked by a common response. Naturally we are always happier when we can celebrate in something joyous and rewarding... but we should never overlook the power of shared sadness. There is something mysterious about the way in which we can share a deep loss or pain. Never be surprised if you see this ultimately buoyant card come up during what appears to be a period of grief and uncertainty.

This 3 is a card whose centre-point is the ability to share, and more than this, to empathise – to enter into the emotions of others without judgement or criticism. It is an accepting and open card which should be encouraging all of us to consider the inter- connectedness of life. When we can each step into the concept that we are one race, one organism, life will change dramatically. No longer will we be able to deny or ostracise the worst elements of our society, and their actions. Instead we will be forced to accept that each and every atrocity committed in this world is committed by some distant part of us; and every triumph achieved by our race-mates is, similarly, achieved by us.

When this card appears with Queens, its specifically "female" qualities are emphasised and filtered according to the Suit of the Queen. So a Disk Queen would bring in practical and almost silent support; a Cup would introduce the insightful and intuitive qualities; a Wand would be contemplating how to put things "right"; and a Sword would observe and probably offer deep and helpful insight. With the Empress, of course, we see all of the self-sacrificial and caring elements to come into play. If the Hanged Man is also close, it is important to consider if events are being assessed efficiently. Here, there is a suggestion that perhaps too much sacrifice is occurring.

This 3 will affirm and strengthen almost any card with which it arises in conjunction. It loves its mates – the other 3s. With a 3 of Disks it will underline practical yet heart-felt projects; with a 3 of Swords we return to the ideas earlier discussed of loss and sadness; with a 3 of Wands, we contemplate the plans we have in place, and welcome their return into our lives.

With the Ace or 2 of Cups, this card can indicate the type of relationship which will last. It also implies that it will be easier than henceforth to heal family rifts, or those gulfs between friends that have caused sadness.

With the Lovers, this 3 indicates a step forward into new and committed territory. With Fortune it allows us to celebrate a triumph with one of our loved ones. With the Star, this 3 assumes its greatest import – we stand a very strong possibility of realising our most deeply treasured hopes and dreams.

FOUR OF CUPS

This card, whilst indicating that there is a lot of love surrounding your querent, can also contain very strong warnings about not taking such precious emotions for granted. It is important that this is picked up when it appears in a reading.

The warning is strengthened when it appears with cards like the Devil, or the Moon, both of which indicate dislocation from reality and a lack of general awareness in certain contexts. This 4 can also be interpreted as a warning if it comes up with blockage cards like the 8 of Swords, the 8 of Cups or the 10 of Wands, when it will imply that energy is blocked and tending toward stagnation. It is possible, at times like these, to be too focussed on what troubles us to make the effort to actively appreciate the loving feelings coming our way.

Thoth Tarot

However, when this card comes up with cards like the 3 or 6 of Cups, with the Empress, Fortune or the Star, we are examining a lovely time in your querent's life. Love is treasured, cherished and reciprocated. With the Lovers you can expect close relationships to move up in the commitment stakes.

It is important to remember that the love that surrounds us does not only come from partners and close family – friends feature strongly when the 4 of Cups is about. It is quite likely that there will be Court cards to indicate the source of the loving feelings.

With cards like the 7 or 8 of Wands you may be looking at a situation where your querent is strengthened by the abundance of care with which they are surrounded, and you would therefore advise that they fall back on this in order to help them face challenge or adversity.

FIVE OF CUPS

Disappointment

Thoth Tarot

Our examinations thus far of the Lord of Disappointment have identified it as a fearsome force in life. It refers to the most dangerous enemy we will ever meet – our Self. For me, this card and the 10 of Swords are probably the worst in the deck. They both point out to us that we are our own most formidable and treacherous foes. And yet, hidden away behind the dire warnings each card brings, is the seed of their own resolution.

It can be very hard to accept that we are infinitely powerful within our own lives. Too often we call ourselves less than we are, too often we surrender without a real fight, too often we dive for the 'victim' cover without considering the consequences. When this card comes up in your reading, it is time to consider what exactly you did to put it there. The cards surrounding this one will help to both rectify the problem, and identify how it came about.

If you see the Moon, 5 of Disks, 7 of Swords or 7 of Cups, these would imply that whatever problem has arisen is mostly rooted in the querent's own belief system. However, remember that the Moon can also indicate lying and deceit – look for Sword Courts, or the 8 or 9 of Swords to try to isolate this effect. The 4 of Cups might also appear to support somebody clouding the truth – this would obviously be strengthened by the appearance of the Moon.

If the 5 of Cups appears with the 10 of Swords, there is deep depression and negativity – probably in the querent themselves. Keep an eye open here for the 8 or 9 of Swords appearing in an 'outside influences' position – this would imply negative interference coming in from outside.

Recovery from the problem might be shown by the Death card (abrupt endings and changes); by Art (bringing opposing forces back into balance); by Aces showing the querent following a new course of action; or perhaps, the Fool, indicating a risk needs to be taken.

The Ace of Wands, Lust and the Sun would all indicate healing, and recovering energies. The Magician would imply that the querent needs to take action themselves. The Universe or the 4 of Wands would indicate that a situation is coming to a satisfactory point of completion.

SIX OF CUPS

This card is a strong one when it appears in a reading. It relates primarily to intimate loving relationships, and to the contentment that arises when we can create one of these for ourselves.

When it comes up with cards like the Sun or the Star, we are looking at a really remarkable situation where the querent's deepest hopes will be satisfied. Here the relationship in question will probably be coming out of a period of trial into a golden time. Remember the 6 of Cups relates to established partnerships which have been ongoing for some time.

Obviously this is a happy and light-hearted card, welcome in any spread. Its influence is intensified if the Lovers

Thoth Tarot

appears, and with the 3 of Cups there is cause for great celebration and joy.

Where it is clear that a relationship has been in trouble – high Swords perhaps - if this 6 appears it will point toward realistic and lasting reconciliation, strengthened even more if the 2 of Cups also comes up.

There are certain combinations which can take the gloss off the card though – it tends to react quite badly to the appearance of either the Devil or the Moon. The Moon will indicate the possibility of deception within the relationship, so here firstly work out whether it is your querent or their partner who is betraying the innate trust usually present with the Lord of Pleasure. If the Devil or the 7 of Cups also appear, the chances are that unfaithfulness is happening somewhere.

On rare occasions this card will come up to indicate an event or activity which is not to do with external relationships, but is more connected with things which lead to a heartfelt sense of being blessed within the querent. This can be connected with many different areas of life – recovery after illness for example. In these cases look for recuperation cards like the Sun or Lust to confirm.

SEVEN OF CUPS

Debauch

Thoth Tarot

This card will never be particularly welcome when it appears in a reading. It indicates at best, weakness and indecision, and at worst, deception, self-delusion and (as its name implies) debauch. As always it is important to examine the cards that surround this one in order to attempt to get a handle on what exactly they are attempting to tell you.

If the Lord of Debauch comes up after cards like the 6 of Wands, the 6 of Disks, the Chariot or the Sun, you need to warn your querent not to squander hard won opportunities. Here they will have invested a good deal of effort in achieving something, and they are then tempted to throw that away for a quick thrill.

If the 7 of Cups were to show with the Hanged Man, or the 7 of Swords, you would be justified in wondering whether perhaps they are caught in an unsatisfying situation that they fear to leave, or to change. The 7 of Disks would point to a more practical environment (like work) but would indicate the same attitude of mind.

If this card appeared followed by the Hermit, or the High Priestess you would be advising a period of withdrawal until they know which choice is best for them. If it were followed by the Ace of Wands, 8 of Wands or Lust, you might advise them that they need to break free of their uncertainty, though you would also be advising against rash action.

If the Lord of Debauch was followed by the 5 or 2 of Disks, caution would be the order of the day again – the wrong choice could lead to material trouble. Followed by the Tower, the cards urge that decisions are made swiftly (especially in the ethical area) before the Universe takes over the deciding.

If cards such as Adjustment (Justice), the Hierophant, a Wand court or the Emperor came up, you would need to warn strongly that they swiftly need to subject their actions to conscientious scrutiny, because they could well be doing something that goes against their regular code of conduct.

With the 8 of Cups, the 7 becomes a very weak card indeed. There is an inability to draw lines in the sand when you get this combination coming up together. This would be further weakened by the appearance of the Hanged Man or the Hermit – here there is an implication that there is something your querent should do that they are avoiding.

Finally, there is a particularly ugly combination that I hope you are fortunate enough never to encounter – the 7 of Cups, with the Devil, and either the 8, 9 or 10 of Swords. This is a group that can indicate (at least) serious sexual misconduct, and at worst, violent sexual behaviour. It would be extremely important if you viewed this combination to identify carefully, from placements and positions, its overall effect.

EIGHT OF CUPS

The Lord of Indolence is a card which speaks volumes about the ways in which we can let ourselves down in life. When this card is relevant we feel overwhelmed, exhausted, and 'all used up'. As a result we can let slide the most basic of personal protections, leaving ourselves wide open to manipulation and abuse.

If the card appears with the 8 of Swords, we may be experiencing pressure and interference from external sources. Look for court cards here to get a sense of where negativity might be flowing from.

With the 7 of Swords, Indolence becomes the victim card – we believe we are unable to effect any change upon our situation. We feel helpless and disempowered. Again look for external sources adding to this effect, but bear in mind that this is much more likely to be a mindset.

Indolence

Thoth Tarot

The Moon does not make a comfortable bed-fellow for the 8 of Cups either, especially if the 7 of Cups is lurking nearby. Here we are probably examining deliberate deception, the possibility of being completely misled. There is an air of trickery in this three-card combination.

With the Devil, the chances are that problems, obstacles and restrictions are self-imposed by failing to maintain adequate and proper boundaries.

However combinations of the Lord of Indolence followed by power cards like the Sun, the Ace of Wands, or the Star, all indicate difficult situations which can be satisfactorily resolved with the application of a bit more strength of character and determination.

If this card comes up with either the Hanged Man or the Hermit following it, more examination of surrounding cards is necessary. It could be that your querent is moving into a period of introspection – essential for throwing off the effects of the 8 of Cups. In this case, you would expect to see encouraging cards later – the 2 of Wands, the 6 of Cups or Swords, or possibly Art.

If, however, this combination is followed by inertia cards – 7 of Swords again, 5 of Swords or Disks - then any process of self-examination undertaken by the querent will fail, leading to more problems along the line.

Learning how to stake out our personal territory is a delicate balancing act which we all need to get the hang of. We need to know where the edges of our selves are. And we need to make these plain to others without impinging on their personal territory. The 8 of Cups is the card which gives us the opportunity to examine these matters carefully and decide whether current arrangements suit us.

NINE OF CUPS

Happiness

Thoth Tarot

This is a lovely card... full of promise and joy. It is called the Lord of Happiness, and it indicates that all is well in life – often on the domestic or emotional front. Generally there is harmony and good forward movement when this card has influence.

If it comes up with the 3 of Cups then the chances are very good that that there will be happy news about a loving relationship moving to a new stage of commitment. The same is true if it appears with the Lovers. With the Ace of Cups, it might signify a new pregnancy which is very welcome, or the beginning of a relationship which will develop great depth and will have, as one of its natural components, a healing effect.

If the card appears with the Star, then it becomes almost magickal, for both of these cards are about making opportunities and then seizing them with determination and drive. If you also see Fortune, then you are looking at an exceptionally successful grouping of cards. With the Magus, the function of Will is strongly underlined.

With the 2 of Cups, you may be examining a reconciliation that brings lasting happiness and contentment. With the 10, you can confidently predict a remarkably satisfying and joyous period.

When the 9 of Cups follows hard cards, like high Swords, Death, the Tower, or the Moon, we see hurtful and distressing circumstances gradually yielding to gentler influences.

There is not much that can dampen this card. It is fairly unusual to see it coming up preceding a bad time, simply because it brings in such light and cheerful influences.

TEN OF CUPS

This is a card which marks happy, peaceful moments in our lives. When writing the Working With section on the 10 of Cups, I suggested that people create quiet spaces in which to simply feel the feeling that this card represents. It is important to savour those moments when we feel at one with the Universe. Every time we do this, we get a little closer to being able to summon the feeling at will.

Thoth Tarot

When this card appears with the Star, the Hierophant or the High Priestess, it will signify important spiritual periods in life. The gates of the unseen have remained open for a little while. We are engaged in a steep learning curve which will probably move us to a higher state of consciousness. They will often be periods where we are studying hard, so look for the 8 of Disks, or the 8 of Wands to indicate the manner of study – Disks would probably indicate solitary study, whereas Wands would suggest communication and learning from others.

If the 10 of Cups appears with cards like the 9 or 10 of Disks, then the influence is more concentrated on home and family life. All is well in this department – life is unfolding in a gentle and loving fashion.

If you see this card in a spread and then more disruptive events follow, the chances are it will be worth warning your querent to be on guard. Do not allow the serenity of this particular moment to blind them to hidden dangers lurking in their path. Cards like Death or high Swords would indicate the nature of the disturbance – for instance, the 8 of Swords would indicate an outside source, whereas the 9 would suggest trouble in the family unit.

If you see this 10 coming up with the 4 or 7 of Cups, pay particular attention to ensure that the contentment and peace is not being taken for granted. Other warnings indicating this might be the 4 of Swords, or even the Tower.

The appearance of the Empress would strengthen the love in the 10 of Cups. This, again, would point to family and home life.

With cards such as the Ace of Wands and the Chariot, you may be examining the sense of achievement that comes when a business project goes well. Look then for the next stages career wise.

PRINCESS OF CUPS

Princess of Cups

Thoth Tarot

Taking into account all that we have already said about the Princess of Cups, you can see that she represents a young woman – or sometimes a child – who is romantic, creative and dreamy.

As you know, when reading Courts, we might be dealing with what we can refer to as the core personality – that is, what a person is at the heart of their being. But we might also be reading changing aspects of a single individual. It is as well to bear this in mind when you draw one of those readings that seems positively over-run with Court cards - look to see if there is a continuous thread running through events and shifts of attitude in order to identify whether you are looking at changing moods.

When this Princess comes up to indicate a mood, rather than a separate person, in most readings she will indicate a woman in the first flush of new love. She demonstrates the 'giddy with excitement' effect that the initial stages of romance can generate. The woman thus indicated will be high on life, filled with a sense of beauty and splendour.

When the woman she indicates is older and more experienced in the ways of the world, this Princess will sometimes imply that the querent is touching areas deep within her which may have been hidden away after hurt and pain have forced her to disassociate from her more romantic nature. If this is the case, keep an eye open for warning cards that might hint of excessive feelings of exposure and vulnerability. Mid-Swords might show this, and high Swords could make you think about whether your querent is actually opening themselves up to dangerous or potentially harmful influences, particularly if you saw the 8 of Cups in the reading too, which would warn that boundaries need to be drawn.

When this card comes up in a reading where the querent has been recently wounded by love, it becomes a little more unpleasant. The Princess of Cups indicates a state of openness – and sometimes lack of objectiveness. She might be seeing a lover through rose-tinted glasses, making too many excuses, refusing to face reality. So long as she remains in this state, she is open to greater pain and harm. Once again, expect the other cards in the reading to give guidance as to how best to help her to protect herself.

PRINCE OF CUPS

The Prince of Cups will represent a young man who is motivated primarily by creative pursuits and matters of the heart. He is a deeply thoughtful, contemplative soul, whose imagination is well developed (and sometimes wildly out of control). His strengths are his gentleness, his vision and his passion. His weaknesses are his lack of focus, lack of direction, and impracticality.

Prince of Cups

Thoth Tarot

When the card appears in a reading, look for surrounding cards that help to round out your view of the personality represented here. If you see cards like the Ace, 6 or 7 of Wands, then you know he is harnessing his creative abilities and skilfully directing them. If you see cards such as the 7 of Swords or Cups, the 5 of Disks or Swords, the 8 of Swords, or the Hanged Man, then you know that he is failing to reach his full potential, that his energies are either dissipated or blocked, and that he will eventually harm his future if he is unwilling to take charge.

If this card comes up to indicate an attitude in an individual, which is a shift from the core personality, then the chances are he is either falling in love, or is impassioned by a particular project. A love affair will be indicated by other Court cards, by cards like the Ace, 2, or 3 of Cups, the Lovers, or the Sun. A project could also come up as an Ace of Cups, but you would expect to also see Wands and possibly Disks to focus on the more practical aspects of the project.

This card most often indicates an actual individual in a reading, rather than moving into the more symbolic realms of interpretation. On the rare occasions when the card appears to mark a situation, rather than a person, it becomes a little more difficult to interpret. In this context, it almost always indicates the flow of supply and demand in a given situation – as you can imagine, this might occur in any area of life. The obvious and most common area of influence, though, is the flow of material wealth in the family arena. We might initially feel that this would be better suited to a Disk card, but in fact, the Prince of Cups develops into the Knight/King of Cups – a figure who reigns supreme in the areas of happy domesticity and close warm loving relationships.

QUEEN OF CUPS

Queen of Cups

Thoth Tarot

As always, when reading court cards, the first thing to decide is whether the card indicates a person, rather than a shift of mood. Some of this will be indicated by the position in which the card appears. Positions relative to the querent (now, hopes and fears, the querent and his/her state of mind) will usually suggest that the court refers to the querent themselves. In positions which are more external (immediate or longer future, what to do, environmental influences) this will usually suggest this is an external person who influences the querent.

The next thing to work out, when reading the Queen of Cups, is whether she is well- or badly-dignified. This will indicate to you the sort of personality you are dealing with. With cards like the Empress, good Cups, or good Wands, you will be dealing with all the very best aspects of this card.

However if you see this Queen come up with cards such as the 7, 8, 9 or 10 of Swords you need to be exceptionally cautious, for here you may be examining the scheming manipulative aspect of the card.

With cards like the Ace and 3 of Cups you are watching the process of a woman falling in love. With high Swords and the Universe you could well be looking at somebody preparing to bring a relationship to an end.

If the Queen of Cups comes up with the Priestess, you may be examining the psychic and intuitive aspects of the card. If the Star also appears then it is possible that enormous spiritual transformation is taking place.

One partnership that tends to indicate future trouble is that of the Queen of Cups with the Knight/King of Swords. Here you will almost always see the potential for a power struggle eventually erupting. The loser would probably be the woman shown as the Queen. Much the same can be said of this card coupled with a man who is represented by the Magus.

Since this Queen can quite easily become detached from reality, you need also to keep an eye open for cards like the Moon, or the 7 of Cups – both of these can suggest that your querent is not living in the everyday world. This effect would be strengthened by the appearance of the Hermit.

KNIGHT OF CUPS

One thing that often confuses readers is how to work out whether a court card represents an individual, an aspect of a person or a mood change. The Queens, by and large, tend to show actual people, but the other three (no matter whether your deck has Kings or Knights, Pages or Princesses) are harder to pin down.

Knight of Cups

Thoth Tarot

The Knight of Cups is an even trickier card than the other Knights, because this card can come up to indicate the personal and loving aspects of a man who, in business for example, might be represented as an Emperor or a Knight of Wands. In order to attempt to pin down an accurate interpretation, look at the surrounding cards.

If you already have a male appearing in the reading, and you notice a shift into the personal area of his life, then you would be justified in reading the card as an aspect of the original man. This would also hold true if you see a man currently troubled (Knight of Swords say) who overcomes a problem in a personal relationship and then turns into the Knight of Cups – his anger has dissipated, and he allows his loving feelings to begin to flow again.

When this Knight represents a single person, he will often come up with cards emphasising his romantic nature – good Cups, or the Lovers. When appearing in his creative aspect, you might expect to see the 3 of Cups, or Art – both cards connected with music, art and literature. Do not be surprised if you also see cards indicating money troubles - unstable Disks perhaps.

As we have already noted, when this Knight goes bad, we will probably see some very dark cards surrounding him. The 9 or 10 of Swords, the Devil, the Moon, or the 7 or 8 of Cups are all strong warning signs that the man in question is sinking toward his own shadow. If in a reading like this, you also see him alternating between the Knight of Cups and the Knight of Swords there is a fair possibility of violent and ugly outbursts. Under these circumstances you would expect the reading to tell your querent what action to take.

SWORDS

ACE OF SWORDS

Ace of Swords

Thoth Tarot

Think of the Ace of Swords as a breath of fresh air – the sharp blade which slices through confusion, uncertainty and doubt. This is a card which tells us we can make the decisions that life demands of us.

Often it will appear after cards indicating a muddled period – 7 or 8 of Swords, 7 or 8 of Cups, 5 of Disks. Look for cards following it that indicate how our actions will better our circumstances, and for cards which indicate which course of action is the best. If the Knight of Wands appears, we would be urged to take swift action, whereas if the Prince of Wands appeared we would be urged toward caution and forethought.

With the Moon, it is possible that the Ace of Swords indicates getting to the bottom of an illusion created by somebody else. Here you would expect to get cards which indicated the perpetrator of this deceit or illusion – Courts probably - and other cards to indicate the area in which the deception is taking place. Cups would suggest romance, Disks business or practical family life, Wands for the interruption of the action of Will.

With cards like the 7 of Swords, the Ace becomes an empowering card. The 7 indicates that we feel unable to make an effectual contribution to life or a given situation, and the Ace tells us to see clearly, look perceptively, and then act on what we find.

If the Ace appeared with the 8 of Swords, the chances are we would find out something that we are not necessarily pleased about, but that will make sense of many things, and also give us a clear path forward.

If this Ace comes up with Adjustment, the chances are we are dealing with matters of justice – legal cases can show this way, as can ethical matters. Sort between the two by looking for cards like the Universe, and other Swords for legal matters, and for lots of Wands, the Sun, the Hierophant, the High Priestess or Lust for matters of ethical concern.

It is especially important if you determine that the Ace is up in an ethical context to look for guidance in the latter stages of the reading. Who is responsible for un/ethical behaviour? How should it be rectified? If your querent is responsible, then you would be looking for cards to indicate that they need to redress the balance – 7, 8, or 10 of Wands could lead you to this conclusion, and if the Tower was up you would be urging them to jump before they got pushed. If it is somebody's else's ethical behaviour causing the problem, expect to see Courts to indicate who, and then read the subsequent cards to work out what the end product would be.

TWO OF SWORDS

Many versions of this card show us a seated woman who is blindfolded, and who holds perfectly balanced swords upright from arms crossed upon her chest. Often there can be water in the background, and also, the Moon sails across the sky. This 2 has very close links with the subconscious and unconscious mind, and these kinds of depictions demonstrate this more clearly than does the Thoth image

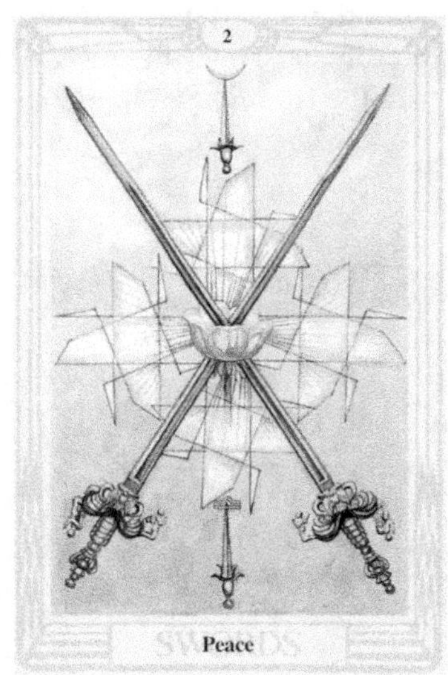

Thoth Tarot

In many respects we humans are driven by impulses and instincts that we do not even think about most of the time. And there is a common denominator to what happens when we do respond automatically, rather than consciously. We tend to make mistakes.

The only way we stand a chance of combatting these blunders is by learning to know, to accept, and to integrate the Shadow Self each of us carries – either as a monkey on the back, or as the revelational Dark Mirror of the Soul. The former is an unknowing state, and the latter an enlightened state.

The Suit of Swords is the rocky path which leads us to self- understanding. And this 2 is the state we achieve when we are able to accept ourselves in entirety – perfect balance and peace.

At a more mundane level, this 2 gives us release and relief when we have passed through the dark indecision of the 3 of Swords, grasped the Ace in both hands and made the choices and decision that we know are right for us.

Sometimes there is an element of delay required in making what seem to be urgent decisions – this might be affirmed by the appearance of the 8 of Disks or the Aeon. Where either of these cards appear, there is an indication that we do not yet have all necessary facts, and should therefore wait until we have greater clarity, avoiding the temptation to revisit the issue until we know what we are dealing with. If the Moon also appears, there is a fair chance we are being deliberately misdirected or deceived.

This 2 does tend to arise after we have been through demanding or argumentative times, and in this context will mark a period where we need to rest and re-evaluate. This will be further emphasised by the 6 of Swords. If it appears with the Hierophant, then we will have received Divine Guidance.

THREE OF SWORDS

Thoth Tarot

Because of some of its darker connotations, The Lord of Sorrow can be an extremely complicated card to read in a spread. Whenever we read a card which could have serious implications for our querent, we need to be exceptionally careful about how we interpret it, and how we convey our interpretations.

As you know, one of the less scary aspects of this card is its indication that a person is having extreme difficulty making decisions. When followed by the 2 of Swords, we can reassure the querent that answers will shortly become clear. When accompanied by the 7 of Swords, or the 5 of Cups, the chances are that the individual is giving themselves a hard time. If the 7 or 8 of Cups appears, then personal boundaries are probably not being maintained. When the 3 appears with the 8 of Swords there's a strong possibility of outside interference causing problems and confusion.

With high Swords, this card becomes a little more menacing. The 9 can indicate external cruelty (or even violence) when coming up with this 3, whereas with the 10, we are probably looking at a seemingly destructive situation which has the seeds of its own resolution contained within it. However on rare occasions the 3 and 10 of Swords can indicate an ugly and damaging situation – look out for the Devil, the Tower or ill-dignified Courts to know whether your querent needs to be warned of impending danger.

One particularly difficult combination that can arise with this card is where it appears just after the Ace of Cups. In certain circumstances the Lord of Sorrow can indicate a miscarriage; since the Ace can show conception, you might be looking at a particularly sad piece of information. If the Ace of Wands shows later, there's some justification for indicating that whilst a pregnancy may be troubled in the early months, later everything will be fine.

Another difficult partnership with the 3 is that of Death. This 3 can indicate loss and grief. If it shows with Death, especially if other cards in the reading support the interpretation, you might be looking at a fatal accident, or other sudden death. The Tower, 10 of Swords, Queen of Swords, or 7 of Swords would all tend to substantiate this divination.

I must include here a word of warning about reading such serious matters – you really do have to be very sure of your ground before you tell a querent you believe there is likely to be a sudden death in their immediate circle. If you are not entirely certain, you would be wise to keep this information to yourself, especially if there is no indication in the reading that positive action could be taken to avert the event.

FOUR OF SWORDS

As we already know this is a card that will come up to mark a period of calm after trauma of one sort or another. To locate the area of trauma, look at past position cards for clues. Ill health will show with high Swords and sometimes the Hanged Man. Emotional harm will show with Death, the Tower, the Universe, or the 5 of Cups. Troubles in the work environment will be indicated primarily by Disks, but sometimes also with Wands (the 10 is quite common here).

When examining the period in front of the querent, look for warning cards like the 7 or 8 of Cups which may indicate blockages to recovery, such as an unwillingness to rejoin the world. If The Hermit also shows, this would therefore pose a strong warning. If the Moon shows in the future, there is a possibility your querent is in denial about events that have taken place. The 8 of Swords would suggest that things are not yet concluded and there is probably more trauma to come. The 9 or 10 of Swords would suggest s/he has not yet come to terms with things, and is unlikely to feel able to move forward. The 10 of Wands might imply that the querent feels blocked – as could the 7 of Swords.

Thoth Tarot

Remember that with the 4 of Swords, there is a tendency to hide away from the world. So when it comes up in a spread, look for cards like the Ace of Wands, the Sun, the 2 and 3 of Wands, to indicate that the querent is gradually moving in a positive and self-affirming way toward adapting to the changes which have taken place. The 7 and 8 of Wands would indicate good forward movement and a sense of self discovery.

The Universe, or Death, in the future after the 4 of Swords would probably indicate that a struggle has not yet been completely overcome. In this case the 4 would show a temporary respite – perhaps in conflict with another person. You would need to look for cards indicating the eventual outcome here, in order that your querent is carefully guided to make the best decisions for themselves – remember, some situations are worth walking away from (check the 10 of Wands to remind yourself of the combinations which may indicate this).

FIVE OF SWORDS

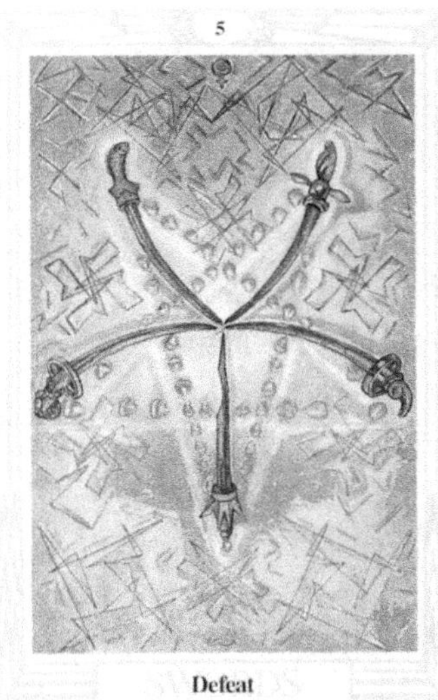

Defeat

Thoth Tarot

This is not a card which will win very many 'most favourite Tarot card' votes but, as is often the case with the cards, it will often indicate a situation to which our own reaction is vital.

The Lord of Defeat points more to our fear of defeat than it does to the reality. So if the card appears with the 8 of Swords, or 8 of Cups, we need to carefully examine our own viewpoints to ensure that we are not painting our world as gloomy as possible. If you do find this is the case, look for cards like the Star, 9 of Cups, or the 9 or 10 of Disks to indicate forward movement and recovery.

With any other 5, this one will tend to indicate difficult periods in life. The 5 of Wands could indicate a conflict with another person which we are unlikely to win; the 5 of Disks may indicate a risky financial course of action; the 5 of Cups will probably indicate an emotional issue which will not easily resolve itself. Remember that 5s are about conflict and confusion, strife and stress which requires considerable effort to overcome.

With high Swords – the 9 and 10 – we are encountering a hazardous period during which we need to be very careful and watchful. If other warning cards such as the Devil or Tower appear your querent needs to be aware that there is considerable threat before them. Look here for cards like the Sun, the Star again, Fortune or the Chariot to indicate how long the hazard will remain.

Where there has been conflict in an emotional situation, the 5 of Swords will indicate a distressing and worrying situation which will cause problems for your querent. Look here for the type of card which would indicate how the problems can best be tackled; the 8 of Wands would indicate that the lines of communication need to be opened, and then remain so, the 8 of Disks would suggest that your querent needs to ensure that they take good care of themselves whilst attempting sort out conflict, and the 8 of Cups would warn against failing to draw adequate boundaries.

When the 5 of Swords appears with Adjustment or the Aeon, there is a possibility that a legal situation will not turn out favourably.

SIX OF SWORDS

The 6 of Swords, Lord of Science, represents a breathing space in the midst of the chaos which is the Suit of Swords. Here we are reminded that if we return to the centre of ourselves all problems, no matter how trying, will eventually find resolution. When we are centred, we can achieve an overview which affords us clarity and peace of mind.

Science

Thoth Tarot

The card indicates that many of the problems which are raised throughout the Suit of Swords are, fundamentally, ours in the making. We effect great influence across our lives, and if we are unwilling to take responsibility for that power then chaos will inevitably ensue.

Therefore if the card comes up with Art, we can be assured that at the centre of ourselves reside the answers we are seeking, and that no other course of action will apply. If these two appear with Adjustment (Justice) then balance and equanimity must be achieved if we are to help ourselves.

With the Moon, the 6 of Swords will show the need to rely on intuition and spiritual guidance to travel through difficult and illusionary times. With

Death it underlines the need for centeredness through change. With the Wheel of Fortune it indicates that you have the opportunity to become the tranquil motionless sphinx at the top of the moving Wheel.

In the deck, this card is preceded by the Lord of Defeat, and followed by the Lord of Futility. These two cards indicate the constant struggle that surrounds the Lord of Science – and its name implies that there is a tried and trusted method of retaining equilibrium, but that this must be learned; it cannot simply be acquired, nor is it naturally occurring. Balancing conflicting forces within and without us is something that comes only with experience and deep contemplation.

When appearing with the Hierophant, the 6 of Swords assumes spiritual proportions – a major learning curve is taking place. This may be demanding and stressful, but will nevertheless result in a wider perspective and deeper understanding. If the Star also appears, the event will be life-changing.

If this card appears with the 5, 7 or 8 of Cups it is time that firm boundaries were established, so as not to invite unfair treatment. With other 6s it creates a stable environment, from which new growth can take place.

SEVEN OF SWORDS

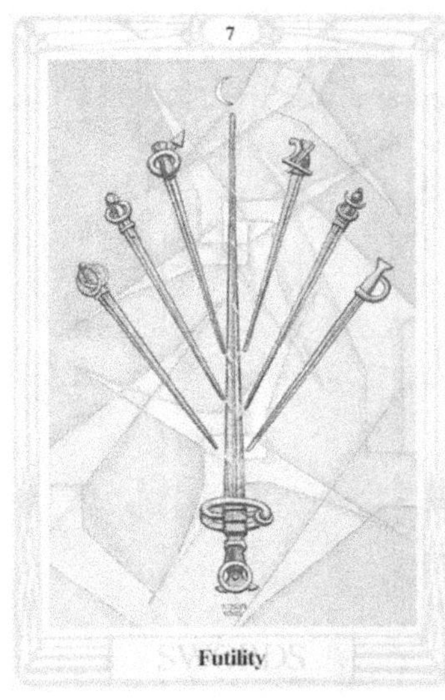

Futility

Thoth Tarot

The Lord of Futility comments more on how we see ourselves than on the reality of any given situation. We feel inadequate and unable to effect a difference – and this, of course, leads us to feel hopeless and doubtful when faced with any form of obstacle or challenge.

When this card appears look for other indications that the problem is primarily an inner faulty belief. The 10 of Wands or Swords, the 5 of Disks or Swords, or Majors like the Devil or the Moon would probably confirm that most of the problems being faced are internal in nature.

Courts, the 8 or 9 of Swords, the Emperor or the Magus may point to external interference, and suggest that the blockage is not within the querent but may be deliberately imposed from outside.

Cards like the 4, 7 or 8 of Cups would imply that there is a certain level of defeatist or victim mentality thinking in play. This will have a negative impact on the eventual outcome.

Following the 7 of Swords, look for action cards which might indicate a method of breaking through the problems surrounding an issue. The Ace of Wands, or Lust, would indicate that matters will yield if a good deal of energy is thrown at them – so you would then advise determined efforts to remove obstacles.

The 8 of Wands would clearly suggest that negotiation and discussion may bring useful results. The 8 of Disks would recommend prudent and thoughtful planning before action takes place. The Hermit, or the Hanged Man, would advise waiting until a clearer picture of circumstances has emerged. A female Cup Court or the Priestess would suggest relying on the psychic and intuitive senses for guidance.

If the Star appears, timing could easily be an issue – matters will not give way until they have achieved their 'rightful' moment. This interpretation would be confirmed by the appearance of the 10 of Cups.

Adjustment or the 6 of Swords would suggest that part of the problem is that your querent does not have a balanced viewpoint on the difficulty, and Art would indicate that they need to attain a centred and steady position within, before they are able to find a resolution.

EIGHT OF SWORDS

The Lord of Interference usually brings in disruption when he appears in a reading. First and foremost, it is important to work out whether you believe that interference is coming from within the querent themselves, or whether it is coming from an outside source.

Inner troubles will be indicated by cards such as the 5 and 7 of Cups – high expectations being disappointed, illusionary attitudes about life being brought into question. The 7 of Swords can be another difficult but internal card, when appearing with the Lord of Interference, showing self doubt and negativity, sometimes so severe as to border on victim mentality. The 10 of Wands would also indicate personal and irrelevant limitations imposed by the querent themselves.

Interference

Thoth Tarot

In these cases look for cards further along in the reading which would show action and determination – both are sometimes required to break through old habit patterns. The 7 or 9 of Wands would indicate that the querent has sufficient inner reserve upon which to draw. The 8 of Wands would suggest that problems will resolve if there is honesty and open communication. The 6 of Swords would imply that if the querent goes for the overview, it will be easier to work out how to make positive progress. Even the Tower could be quite good (if a bit disturbing) here, because of its ability to push us forward even when we hesitate. In this case, look for cards like the Sun, Fortune, the Fool, the Star or the Ace of Wands to indicate how things will eventually work out when the querent is making the effort.

To determine that the Lord of Interference indicates external intrusion into a person's life is something about which the reader must be quite thorough. When this card comes up to reveal another person's intentions, it almost always points to malicious and conscious intervention by a third party. Therefore it is usually quite a serious event in the querent's life, and might indicate ill-wishing and bad feeling.

Look for Courts to represent other people. Keep an eye open for anything which might reveal their motives. And above all, look for cards which offer some kind of solution to the problem. You might find cards like the Tower here, too – and possibly the 8 of Wands, if confrontation is required. But you would also expect to find cards such as the 4 of Swords, to indicate an uneasy peace, or the 3 or 4 of Disks, to indicate justified effort and adherence to ethical beliefs.

If either the 10 of Swords or the 10 of Wands, comes up with this card, advise your querent to back away slowly. This is a situation which can only be made worse by expending energy upon it. Do not be surprised to also find cards like Death here, advising a complete break from the given situation. The Devil and this 8 make a bad combination too, for they can, together, tend to pull a person away from their own principles, and lead them to act in a fashion they would not customarily agree with.

The Moon with the Lord of Interference can suggest that, not only is your querent subject to outside pressure, but that the pressure being applied is being deliberately concealed. Acts of deceit are likely in this situation. Look for the High Priestess or the Princess of Cups – both cards which recommend your querent relies on their own intuition.

NINE OF SWORDS

Thoth Tarot

The first thing to decide when faced with a reading containing the 9 of Swords is whether the cruelty indicated is self-created by the querent, or whether it is coming from an outside source.

To show that unkindness is internal, look for cards like the 5, 7 or 10 of Swords, the 7 of Cups, or possibly the 5 of Disks. Look also for cards which explain why your querent would feel so bad about themselves that they would want to inflict this level of pain, and also for cards which indicate methods by which they can heal from the distress they feel.

Cruelty coming from an external source might well show with the 8 of Swords, the Devil, some Courts (most likely Swords), 8 of Cups or perhaps the Tower. In this situation you need first to look for consequences – Death, the 2 of Disks, the Moon, or the 5 or 10 of Wands would give you clues as to the effects. The first two would suggest that established and accepted conditions will change as a result of another person's actions. The Moon would indicate deliberate deception. The two Wands would show conflict and oppression.

One particularly unpleasant combination, which thankfully rarely comes up, would be the 9 of Swords, the 8 of Cups, the Devil and the 10 of Swords. This grouping could indicate that your querent is at serious risk and needs to remove themselves immediately from the situation.

Whenever you are attempting to read a card like the 9 of Swords, look to the future cards for indications of how best to deal with the effects. If necessary draw three more cards to attempt to clarify the effects of the Lord of Cruelty. Sometimes this allows you to clarify the event or situation indicated, and this could be a useful tactic with other difficult cards too, like the 3 of Swords for example.

Cards like the Sun or Lust (Strength) would show that the querent can, and will, pull out of the position which is causing problems and achieve a happier balance in their life. Cards such as the Universe or the 4 of Wands would clearly show that a bad situation needs to be brought to a conclusion. The 8 of Swords may indicate waiting until matters become clearer before taking action. Strong Courts would suggest that the querent needs to be more dynamic in their handling of events.

TEN OF SWORDS

This tends to be a 'whaa' card when it turns up in a reading. But as we have already discovered, it is a card with a strong message about creating our futures the way that we want them to be. How do we find out whether the Lord of Ruin appears as a warning about our own approach to life, or whether its appearance presages a nasty event? We check the cards surrounding it.

Thoth Tarot

If, in the past area of a reading, you find cards like the 5s of any suit, or the 8 of Swords, the 7 of Cups, or the 10 of Wands, you already know that your querent has some sort of blockage. If there is no sign of attempts to resolve that problem – 8 of Wands, 8 or 9 of Disks, 6 of Cups or Wands - then there is a fair chance the 10 of Swords will be an 'outcome' card, rather than a warning card.

If the Lord of Ruin appears with other external influence cards, like the Tower, Death, the Universe, the Star or possibly one of the Aces, again the chances are that life is about to deal a nasty blow. Here, though, the 10 could be marking the way in which the querent needs to deal with whatever upcoming event occurs.

With cards like the Hermit, Art, or the 8 of Disks in the future, the 10 is more likely to be a warning. You need to advise your querent to go within and carefully examine their own personal attitudes. This is further underlined if the Priestess is present.

With the Devil, especially when accompanied by the 9 of Swords you might well be looking at a really serious and violent situation. I have seen these three, with the 7 of Cups come up to indicate impending rape, and reversed Sun to indicate a violent street attack. If you are ever unfortunate enough to be faced with a reading of this type, you would be well advised to run a second reading to check outcomes and whether the situation can be avoided. If you select the cards causing concern and set them aside from the deck, you can then concentrate your attention on them, and reshuffle asking something like "Give me more information about the circumstances of this event." You should get a fairly helpful indicator about how your querent needs to handle themselves.

As a matter of interest, in the case of the rape, I 'felt' it would be a sexual assault, but said that I believed my querent may be placed in a very dangerous situation. There was also a male Court card up whom at the time she could not identify. Three weeks later a colleague asked her to go out for a drink after work, and she almost accepted, then remembered the reading and refused. He took objection to her refusal and never spoke to her thereafter. Two months later he was dismissed from his job after attempting to force himself on another woman at work.

The 10 of Swords is not an easy card to read. You are almost always going to be telling your querent something that they do not want to hear. However, it is your duty to convey, as best you can, what the cards are telling you, and then find ways of assisting the querent in making the best of what could be a bad situation.

PRINCESS OF SWORDS

Princess of Swords

Thoth Tarot

As with the other Princesses, before you can interpret the Princess of Swords properly, you need to determine whether the card represents an actual person, a mood in a person not normally associated with this Princess, or an idea.

To do this look at the cards surrounding this one, and consider your own responses. Position can be a giveaway as to whether this is another person – card positions such as outside influences and environment will more likely indicate that the card shows a person. In hopes and fears, or dreams and ambition type placements this card will often show an idea or intention. In positions which allow you to see more of the querent, she may represent a shift of mood.

If you see either a person or shift of mood indicated by the Princess of Swords, look for other high Swords in order to tell you whether this is a particularly dangerous version of the Princess. She can sometimes come up to indicate a person so sunk in their own unhappiness that they can turn viciously upon those around them. In this case you need to identify whether she represents your querent – in which case a warning is in order - or alternatively, she may represent somebody who can impact against your querent – different type of warnings applicable here.

The Princess sometimes shows a person with a rebellious nature, who is given to challenge and conflict. One especially interesting placement comes up when this card appears with the Hierophant. Because the Hierophant indicates (among many other things) the established order, or way of things, this combination would tell you that somebody is deliberately challenging some sort of institution – a bit of a David and Goliath type situation. Keep an eye open for cards which suggest whether the current rebellion will be successful.

It is a peculiarity of the Swords females that when you get the two of them up in a reading they will most often indicate a mother/daughter partnership. This is not true, in my experience, with any of the other suits – even though it should be.

As an enemy this Princess is second only to the Queen of Swords as a nasty piece of work. If you sense within a reading that the darker side of the Princess is showing, keep a close eye open for cards like the 7 or 8 of Swords, the 8 of Cups and the Moon. Any combination of these could indicate duplicity or downright malice.

I do have to say that when a person has attracted the negative attentions of a Sword female the most effective remedy will be to get out of that person's sphere of influence and stay out – women who have developed the Sword energy have exceptionally long memories.

PRINCE OF SWORDS

This card will most usually come up in a reading to indicate a male having influence in the querent's environment. It may indicate an intelligent, quick witted young man who is, by his very nature, articulate and insightful.

The card might also, under certain circumstances, come up to indicate the mood of a young man connected to your querent. In this case, this Prince becomes somewhat more uncomfortable, for there will often be intense anger and disquiet when somebody is going through these kind of mood swings.

If it is the latter, look for cards which tell you exactly what effect the emotional atmosphere will have. With cards like the

Prince of Swords

Thoth Tarot

9 of Swords, the Devil, or the Tower, there's a real danger of things getting out of hand. Deliberate cruelty, malice and deceit are possible here – even, at worst, violent outbursts and volatile situations could erupt.

If you sense that it is this kind of Prince of Swords you have come across in a reading, look for cards to analyse your querent's response. The 7 or 10 of Swords would suggest they feel victimised and helpless, whereas Death would imply impending change in the general situation, and may also represent advice to your querent – suggesting that if the situation is not brought to a proper conclusion, the effects will be serious.

Less often, this Prince will come up to indicate a particular type of energy, which is very fast- flowing – quicksilver in its delivery of ideas and solutions. You would identify this if the Ace of Disks or Wands was present, and especially if the Star appeared close by. In this situation, pay special attention to the advice given by the cards. Action cards like the Emperor, Lust or good Wands would suggest your querent must act swiftly and decisively upon their ideas, for example.

QUEEN OF SWORDS

Queen of Swords

Thoth Tarot

One of the tricky things to sort out, when this card comes up in a reading, is whether it identifies a woman whose core personality is that of the Queen of Swords, or whether it shows a woman who has recently suffered loss (or is in some other way ill-dignified).

Sometimes this card can indicate that a particular person has ill-intent toward your querent for some reason. Obviously it is important to be able to sort out which type of Queen you are looking at.

Some of this comes from the actual placement of the card in the reading. Any external position – external influences, matters beyond the querent's control, the matter immediately confronting the querent - could indicate an external female, who is either harbouring ill- will toward the querent, or has recently been widowed or separated from her partner.

When the card comes up in more internal positions – hopes and fears, the now, the past - then the card will often represent the querent. At this stage you need to work out whether this is a core personality, or a particular reaction to events surrounding her.

If the Queen comes up around high Swords, the Tower, Death or the Universe, the chances are that the card indicates a transient effect. Look for other Queens to give you an idea as to the querent's core personality. The different suits will sometimes give you clues as to how she might deal with what she has experienced. A Queen of Cups core personality will tend to be very emotionally damaged by distressing experiences. A Disk will tend toward tackling practical matters. A Wand might react defiantly, showing the world she can cope. Somebody who was a core Queen of Swords passing through painful times will either go for the high ground of logic, or sink to the morass which is her dark side.

If you determine that the Queen represents an external person who harbours ill-will, you need to find cards like high Swords again, 7 or 8 of Cups, the Devil, 3 of Swords, 5 of Wands to confirm your interpretation. Look also for cards which would suggest a solution to the problem.

If she appears to represent an outside female who is currently grieving, then you may find Death or the Universe coming up in the reading. In this case you need to be looking for cards that indicate whether the querent needs to take action on the Queen's behalf.

KNIGHT OF SWORDS

When we encounter the Knight of Swords in a reading, it is important to determine whether we feel the card indicates an attitude or a person. This decision dictates how the card is read.

If we feel that the card represents an attitude then we must expect a period of lightning quick thought, flexibility, mind-changing and communication. Look for cards like the 8 of Wands, the 9 of Disks and the Death card to try to narrow down in what field the intellectual activity will take place. If the card is followed by an Ace (though not normally the Ace of Cups) we must expect that the movement signalled by the Knight's appearance will happen under the aegis of the suit the Ace comes from.

Knight of Swords

Thoth Tarot

For instance, if he was followed by the Ace of Disks, we would look to business, material and financial affairs to indicate what kind of ideas will come up. If it was followed by the Ace of Swords we would expect logical, philosophical or possibly occult leaps forward. If it was the Ace of Wands that emerged, we may be looking at acts of conscious Will, or perhaps the following of a heart-felt desire.

You will normally find surrounding cards which indicate what influence these events would have. Cards such as the Sun, 6 of Disks or 6 of Wands would indicate easy success. Cards like the Tower, 2 of Disks or Death would indicate breakthrough past obstacles into new areas. With Adjustment or the Universe, you may well be dealing with legal or contractual matters, and again you would look for confirmation cards to indicate progress.

On the other hand, if the card comes up followed by more negative cards – like the 5 of Disks or Wands, or the 7 of Cups - you would be predicting that the outcome of events is not going to be terrifically favourable. In this case, look for cards that indicate courses of action that could be taken to minimise effects.

If you decide that the card indicates a person, then you must first decide whether this Knight is showing a man who is, at heart, a Knight of Swords. If so, then expect to find him relatively elusive where love and commitment are concerned – a little unreachable, more willing to solve emotional matters by the use of logic than anything else.

If you feel that the card represents a man who has adopted, for a time, the dark side of the Knight of Swords, then you will find cards like the Moon (to indicate treachery), the Devil (to indicate manipulation), or the 7, 8, 9 or 10 of Swords (to indicate mistreatment of others). If you are in the unfortunate position of reading for a man who shows in this fashion, can I just warn you to choose your words carefully – he does not make the best of enemies.

DISKS

ACE OF DISKS

Ace of Disks

Thoth Tarot

As you know this card will often signify the start of a new project or business venture. Look for cards like the 6 of Wands or Disks to indicate good progress and a successful conclusion. The Sun would be another beneficial card to follow the Ace.

The 7 of Disks might indicate initial problems, possibly signalling delays or blockages. The 2 of Disks could imply that things will get off to a rather shaky start. But if the Ace of Disks came up with a card like the Tower, or Death, you might want to suggest to your querent that they choose a different direction, because these cards would suggest that the project is unlikely to succeed.

If the Ace was accompanied by other Aces, it would be worth looking at whether these tell you something about the project itself – for instance the Ace of Cups following the Ace of Disks would indicate that the querent has a good deal of emotional investment in the work involved, so it might be a creative project.

If the Ace of Disks appears with the 3 of Cups and the Empress, this shifts the meaning of the card a little and may indicate a pregnancy. This combination can also occasionally apply to the birth of young from any creature.

The Ace of Disks can also sometimes indicate sudden inputs of wealth – lucky wins, legacies or investments maturing. You can tell the difference here by looking for the Wheel of Fortune for luck, the Death card for legacies and the Universe for investment.

TWO OF DISKS

This card indicates changes of fortune. As I have said before, if you remain inert and refuse to allow change to take place, you may well eventually experience the effects of the Tower, when you are thrown head-long into life, and change is imposed upon you whether you like it or not.

When the 2 of Disks appears in a reading, look at what surrounds it to try to assess where its effects will be felt. If it is accompanied by other Disks, then the changes it indicates probably will be found in the practical, working or financial areas. One combination to keep your eyes open for is the 2 and 10 of Disks together – this almost always indicates a change of residence. With the Ace it would point to a

Change

Thoth Tarot

new project beginning, perhaps a new job. With the 4 or the 6 of Disks we would be reassured of the successful completion of whatever is currently going on.

If this card appears with Wands, we might still be looking at the career area of life, but we would know that the occupation was very close to the querent's heart. It would assume greater status than being 'just a job'. With the Ace of

Wands it is possible you are looking at an unexpected and unplanned pregnancy (look for the Ace of Cups to indicate the birth). With the 4 a project needs to be brought to proper completion so that change and forward movement can begin. With the 5 or 10 of Wands, we may be looking at a change of attitude to a given problem, and its subsequent resolution.

With Cups, we would tend more toward the family and loving areas of life. Here the 2 of Disks becomes more intimate and personal. With hard Cups like the 5, 7 or 8 we might be advocating major changes in the ways relationships work. With the 2 or the 3 we would feel that a given situation was changing for the better.

If this card appears with Swords, its effects tend to be a little more harsh. The airy power of Swords implies that change should already have taken place, and the fact that it has not is causing damage to the querent's life. With the 3, 5, 7, 8, 9, and especially, the 10, change is absolutely imperative if circumstances are to improve. However if the 2 of Disks appears with the 2 of Swords, this allows a shift of perspective that will bring spiritual contentment and peacefulness.

THREE OF DISKS

Thoth Tarot

The Lord of Works shows us that steady dedication to a task will complete it efficiently and satisfactorily. Some versions of the card show illustrations of a master craftsman at work. And the card can sometimes come up in a reading to signify mastery of a given skill. When it appears with the 8 of Disks, with Art (Temperance) or with the 6 of Wands you might look for this kind of interpretation.

Although the 3 of Disks can come up to indicate any form of concerted effort in the work or study arena, it can also come up to indicate tasks which have a great deal of meaning to the querent. Heartfelt passions in the creative and working fields will be indicated by a combination of Disks and Cups. You will often also find quite a few Majors around the card when it indicates inspired tasks. Look carefully at the Cups – they may indicate impending problems. For instance, if the 5 came up, you'd be wondering whether your querent hasn't been disappointed by unfulfilled first expectations. If the 7 came up, then perhaps they tend to hesitate rather than getting on with things. The 8 would imply laziness or lack of deliberate effort, which would cause conflict with the diligence of the 3 of Disks.

If the Lord of Works came up with the Chariot, the Sun, or other positive and energetic cards, such as the 6 of Wands you would be able to assure your querent that their efforts were going to lead to success.

Cards like the Hierophant or the High Priestess, together with the 8 of Disks, might lead you to consider that the querent is undertaking some kind of study when reading the 3 of Disks. The two Majors are both teaching cards. Cards like the 6 of Wands, the Universe or the 4 of Wands would indicate a successful outcome.

If this card came up with more disruptive cards like the Tower or the 8 of Swords, you would need to examine the reading for indications as to whether there was outside interference, or whether, your querent's activities were crossing other people's boundaries. This is because not only does this card cover dedicated effort in business, it also covers the kind of activities best described as "good works". Sometimes a person can think they are acting in the best interests of some-one else, but their behaviour may be interpreted as interfering from the other side of the fence.

FOUR OF DISKS

This card has a somewhat bad reputation among some commentators on the Tarot. Whilst I can see why, I don't necessarily agree. In our last examination of the 4 of Disks we talked about how the card can indicate a certain stagnation of energy – when we try to hold on to material and mundane things too tightly they lose the essential flow which is a natural part of life. And it is upon this rigidity that some people concentrate.

However this card can make a positive contribution in certain situations – when things are very chaotic, for instance, it will indicate an active effort to impose order and forward-planning. Such deliberate processes of organisation will often bring a muddled situation to some sort of stability.

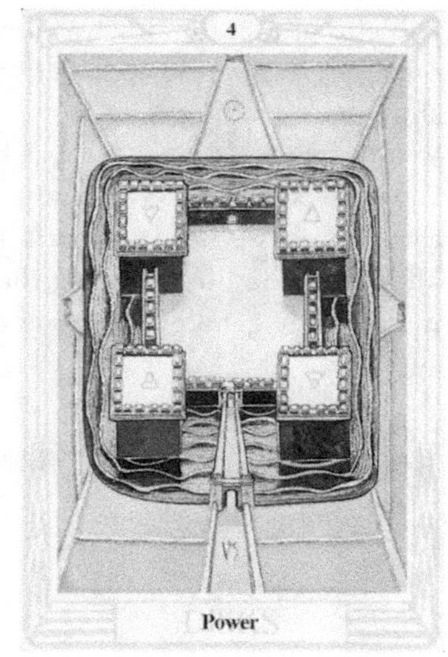
Power

Thoth Tarot

As we have observed before, though Disks do relate to money, work and material things, they also reflect the everyday matters in life – family, home, overall security. So sometimes the 4 of Disks will come up in a reading which generally talks of, say, a strained emotional relationship, along with midrange Cups, and mid to high Swords. In this case it would indicate that the querent needs to return to practicalities – the situation has become too clouded by confusion, frustration, or high emotional trauma. It is time to impose some order, and to deal with daily practical matters, thus allowing things time to calm down. Look also for cards like the 7 of Disks to indicate whether there is also some threat of financial damage if they do not pay attention.

Another aspect of this card that sometimes comes up stems from its relationship to Chesed, as we discussed in the 2nd Edition of the Tarot Guide. You may remember that Chesed is the point at which pure energy starts to convert into form. Imagine that you are at the very start of making or building something. If your very first steps toward its manifestation are not properly thought out, the eventual product will be flawed, because it is built on flawed foundations.

So when reading the 4 of Disks always bear in mind that, at one level, this card relates to our innermost moral attitudes towards money and material matters. If our thoughts and feelings here are not positive and clear, we are liable to attract to ourselves unwelcome influences that filter down to affect our lives. You would consider opting for this definition when legal problems show in a reading (Universe, Adjustment/Justice), when you see inputs of wealth which occur quite quickly (Ace, 6, or 10 of Disks) or when readings show exceeding good fortune regarding material matters (Fortune, Star). In these cases, we need to carefully assess our attitudes toward money, wealth and mundane life, ensuring that we are clear in our objectives, pure in our motives, and generous with our abundance.

FIVE OF DISKS

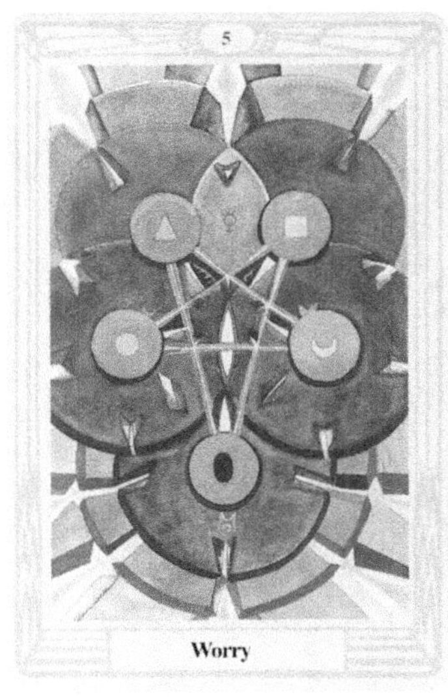

Thoth Tarot

As we have said often in our discussions of the 5 of Disks, this card represents anxiety about imagined or real impending events which we believe will impact upon our material, financial or family life. When it turns up in a reading there are two things you need to look out for – which area of life is likely to be affected, and whether the perceived threat is real or not.

To work out which area will be affected, bear the following in mind – material life will tend to produce quite a broad spread of cards, including Disks, Wands, and sometimes mood cards like high Swords or Cups, whereas financial matters will be more likely if the Lord of Worry is primarily accompanied by other Disk cards. And family matters will often not show with Disks, but with a fair sprinkling of Cups and Swords.

In order to work out how much of a threat really is posed, you need to examine the cards close to the 5, especially time-wise immediately after it appears. Real threats will be marked by hard cards – 7 of Disks, 10 of Swords,

Death, or the Tower. When you find these in a reading, look further on to try to glean some guidance in coping with a situation which is liable to cause considerable disruption in your querent's life. Cards such as Fortune or the Star could indicate one of those life-changing moments where, through adversity, the querent takes up challenges they would not otherwise have chosen. The Ace of Disks could indicate new working opportunities, and sometimes large sums of money. The Ace of Wands might indicate the start of a new project which is 'heartfelt'.

If, when this 5 appears, you see cards like the 7 of Swords, urge your querent not to give up. This advice would be further supported if the 7 or 9 of Wands came up too, indicating that they must draw on reserves of inner strength in order to deal with their fears.

With the Devil, the 5 of Disks would indicate that fears must be squarely faced and challenged. With the Universe or the 4 of Wands, whether it seems like it or not, a phase is coming to a natural conclusion, allowing for new development and growth.

With the Hermit, the Lord of Worry could indicate an unhealthy withdrawal from reality – look for cards like the 9 of Swords to confirm this. However, if the 5 and the Hermit were accompanied by, say, Art or the Chariot, moving from one unhelpful situation to a more positive one is indicated.

SIX OF DISKS

The Lord of Success is a welcome card in most readings, indicating that hard work and perseverance have paid off. This is especially strengthened if it follows the 3 of Disks – showing applied effort, or 8 of Disks which could suggest hard study paying off. If it follows the 4 of Wands then a stage of completion has been achieved, leading to success and good fortune.

If this card is followed by the Sun, we would be confident that ambitions are being successfully fulfilled. If the Star comes after it in a reading, then we can be assured that the highest dreams and aspirations of the querent are likely to be satisfied.

Thoth Tarot

With cards such as the Emperor, we would feel that an entrepreneurial triumph has been achieved. However if the card appeared with the Empress we would be turning our attention to home-life and family, seeking out a success in that area – this combination could indicate a woman who has pride in the accomplishments of their family members.

With the 6 of Wands, we would tend to regard the success as more unplanned – a breakthrough after considerable resistance has been encountered. If the card appears with the 9 of Disks, then material success will probably be ongoing. The 10 of Disks would remind your querent that wealth, if it is to flow, must be used. Wealth, like any other energy, stagnates when standing still.

When this card appears with a court card, it will very often indicate success in the life of an individual who is important to your querent. Try to pin down who this is in order to expand on the reading.

The 6 of Disks following the 2 of Disks would suggest a change of material status, after a struggle. This would be further confirmed by the appearance of cards like the Chariot or the Wheel of Fortune.

This card rarely indicates sudden windfalls, or unexpected influxes of funds. It usually refers to material changes which have been planned and worked toward.

SEVEN OF DISKS

Failure

Thoth Tarot

The Lord of Failure will come up in a reading to indicate one of two options. Either there is some real failure on the horizon – we will not get that job we applied for, we will not pass our exams, our business interests will stagger – or it shows our own fears around money, material matters and personal security. The only way to work out which of these two applies is to study the cards which surround it.

With the former interpretation – the real event – you would be looking for cards to pin down the severity of the matter in hand. The 5 of Disks would imply quite serious problems, but ones which can be overcome with effort. The 9 of Disks would also imply that more effort needs to be invested, but offers a more promising outcome. The 2 of Disks would suggest that a change of direction was necessary in order to re- establish harmony. This would be further underlined by cards like Death, the Universe or the 4 of Wands.

With the latter interpretation – showing the querent's fears rather than an actual failure - you will probably find other cards which indicate fears and worries. For instance you might see the 7 of Swords, or the 8. These would tend to indicate inner discomfort and turmoil. Look also for cards like the 10 of Wands – these would suggest that the querent feels unable to get past obstacles and blockages.

When the 7 of Disks comes up with Cups, you are more likely to be examining the emotional side of family and domestic life. With cards such as the 5 or 7 of Cups, high expectations have been disappointed, or hopes dashed. If this card appears after the 2 of Cups, a reconciliation might fail. Followed by the Universe or Death, the relationship will inevitably break down.

A mix of Cups and Wands, on the other hand, can often be quite hopeful on the family front. If this 7 appears with, say, the 2 of Cups and the 8 of Wands, communication will clear confusion, and difficulties will be resolved. The 5 of Cups with the Lord of Failure presents quite a dark picture in which hope seems to have fled... but with the Star, or the Ace of Cups following, difficulties can be overcome.

EIGHT OF DISKS

The Lord of Prudence is an interesting card and has three major areas of relevance – one is as advice on the general financial situation, another is related to learning new skills, and finally, this card can indicate a period of spiritual or emotional growth which takes its toll on health and energy.

Spiritual development can be marked by several tarot cards – most notably the Priestess, the Hierophant, the Moon and the Star. Sometimes the Ace or 10 of Cups will also appear.

But when the 8 of Disks is also present in a reading you have determined is of a spiritual nature, it is important to take a good look at the cards surrounding it. The

Thoth Tarot

Lord of Prudence can sometimes offer warnings to conserve energy, to be less intense about our efforts. And with some cards – the 7 of Cups most notably – it can represent a very strong warning that growth is taking place too fast.

It may seem strange to suggest that spiritual growth can occur too quickly – but in truth this is quite a common phenomenon. Once a person's imagination is caught up in the unseen world, they can begin to lose touch with everyday reality. This can lead to eventual disassociation and separation. This scenario would be indicated by the appearance of cards like the Moon, and possibly the Devil. Cards like the 9 or 10 of Swords would indicate the possibility of a serious breakdown.

The 8 of Disks can come up in a spiritual reading to indicate things other than warnings though. It also speaks to us about the principle of service, which is central to any successful spiritual growth. In order that we are able to step into, and engage, the energies of this Universe of ours, we must be willing to absorb and learn, and we must also be willing to emanate and teach. This is part of our unspoken contract with the High Powers. What we take we must replace.

The Lord of Prudence also points to an important learning tool – the repetition of routine tasks frees the mind and allows an open connection with spirit. The Rider Waite version of this card sums up well the concept of repetition. A craftsman sits beneath a tree, carving pentacles into wood. Beside him, up the trunk of the tree, are all the pentacles he has carved before. He is lost in the process of carving – a skill with which he is completely familiar.

His concern is for each shaving of the wood, each sweep of the tool in his hand. He concentrates solely on this one repetitive task, and as a result, he has 7 finished pentacles ready to find their new owners, and he is working on the eighth.

By concentrating on a familiar task, but undertaking it with intent, we release our own powers of creation. The mind, at liberty for a time, will fly to the high ground, and quite possibly bring back new outlooks, perceptions and realisations.

NINE OF DISKS

Thoth Tarot

This is a welcome card to show in a reading. At a mundane level it indicates incremental gain and growth, and at an arcane level it talks of the soul's ability to make its presence felt more clearly in everyday life.

If it appears with the Ace of Disks you can rest assured that new projects will begin which will lead to greater material stability and ease. If it comes up followed by the 10 of Disks, remember that accumulated wealth must be allowed to flow unrestricted in order to continue to develop.

With other 9s this card indicates that the querent is on the threshold of achieving a given set of aims – look for 10s, the 4 of Wands or the Universe to indicate that the goal has been achieved.

Disks can also relate to the domestic life of your querent, so if you feel this card has come up to indicate some natural progress on that front, look out for the Ace of Wands which would show changes of lifestyle, or the Ace of Cups which might indicate a new member of the family.

Oddly this card rarely comes up with bad Swords. The 7, 8, 9, and 10 of Swords do not often come up in combination with this 9. If, on occasion, it does happen, it will generally indicate that whilst the emotional side of things is causing problems, the more mundane and everyday aspects of life are going well.

If the 9 of Disks follows the 8 of Disks, then often you are examining a period where the querent comes out of a study phase and begins to apply their learned skills, perhaps in their job.

This card also relates to the concept of just rewards. When it appears there has always been ongoing effort before the success symbolised by this 9. Look for cards like the 3 or 4 of Disks, the 6 of Wands, and the 6 of Swords to give you an idea of what kind of success has been achieved. Disks would indicate the workplace, or material matters; Wands could indicate private enterprise, and Swords would tend to point more to inner struggles and conflicts finding eventual resolution.

TEN OF DISKS

This card is generally welcome in a reading, though if it comes up in a past position, keep an eye open for signs that the initial wealth indicated has been in some way diminished. The 3 of Swords, Tower or Death might show that this is the case.

One particular theme that will often be marked by this card is the buying and selling of property. Look also for movement cards like the Ace of Disks, the Knight of Wands (movement) or cards which indicate upheaval, as well as 'legal' cards like the 8 of Disks or Adjustment (Justice) to indicate dealing with contracts.

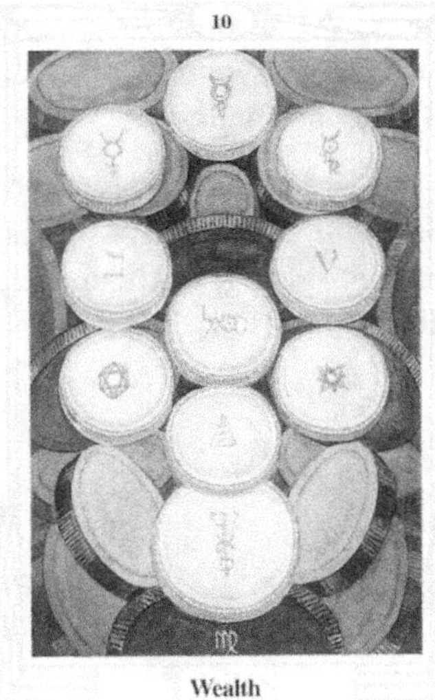

Wealth

Thoth Tarot

Another aspect of the 10 of Disks is its reference to people who are becoming complacent. You would expect to see perhaps the Hanged Man, 4 of Cups or 7 of Cups appearing close by. In this circumstance look also for cards which indicate how the querent would best resolve their problem before it causes trouble. If, in the reading, the 'solution' cards turn up before some unpleasant event, then by rectifying the initial attitude the querent may be able to avert the eventual outcome. So if you found (for instance) the 8 of Disks or the

Chariot just after the group of cards surrounding the 10, then you would advise that it is prudent for the querent to take a close look at their attitudes, and value what they have, rather than taking it for granted.

This card relates to established wealth, rather than growing abundance, or sudden good fortune. The security reflected by it has been built up over years of steady effort. So if you see the 10 of Disks followed by cards like the 9 or 10 of Swords, there is a threat to the status quo – probably from an outside influence. Advise against taking risks, making investments and so on during the period affected.

If you saw this 10 come up with the 4 of Disks you would need to consider whether there's a possibility your querent is becoming too entrenched in material security, allowing this to shape their attitudes. Look for cards to indicate how things can be livened up and taken to a higher level. Cups would show that clear contact with the emotions needs to be established. Disks might suggest a change of direction at the material level. Swords would indicate that it is the thought pattern of the querent that needs to be tackled... perhaps there are faulty ideas around security and wealth which could usefully be challenged.

With cards like Art (Temperance), the Universe and the Star, this is a very fortunate card to have appearing in a reading. Stability has been achieved. Life unfolds rightfully, and the querent is receiving the just reward for his/her efforts.

PRINCESS OF DISKS

Princess of Disks

Thoth Tarot

As already noted, this card can indicate pregnancy – you would be looking for either the Princess of Cups, or possibly the Ace of Cups, to indicate conception, and for the Ace of Wands to mark the new arrival.

When this card appears in a reading with the Chariot, we are observing a period of diligent preparation before setting off on a significant course of action. The beginning of University life, leaving home, a marriage or other dramatic and important life change may show this way.

When she comes up to indicate a mood, rather than an event or person, the Princess of Disks will indicate practical activity aimed at producing order. This will be especially beneficial if you see cards indicating earlier confusion, since the Princess draws in earthy stable energy.

Sometimes – though more rarely – this card comes up to indicate good news in the material field. You would need cards such as the 9 or 10 of Disks, the Sun, or Fortune to confirm this interpretation.

At her very core, the Princess of Disks is well-rooted and reliable, intent on creating a harmonious and calm environment. She can sometimes come across as reserved or quiet, though this is something of a misconception. Whilst she surely does not waste her words, she is quite passionate about supporting the things she sees to be 'rightful' in life. She is a keen proponent of family values, and tends to clearly practice what she preaches. Whilst it may sometimes appear that her horizons seem quite narrow, this is more a matter of her intent focus than a comment upon her intellectual abilities. She has the remarkable skill of aiming all her attention in one direction at a time.

If you observe a querent becoming Princess of Disks immediately before exams, or test periods, you can be sure she is going to be absolutely singular in her focus till her task is done. This will also occur when indicating a person intent on finishing a creative project – almost to the level of obsession in some cases. This can be good if the core personality is slightly unfocussed, like the Princess of Cups, but can be overbearing and intolerable when applied, for instance, to the Queen of Swords.

PRINCE OF DISKS

This is a quietly forceful card – it embodies unfailing and determined self direction toward perceived goals. The Disk males can sometimes be a little misunderstood, for on the surface, they appear calm and steady – lacking in fiery excitement and grace. Yet this is a short-sighted interpretation of the card, especially when examining a well-rounded version of the type. Disks are, indeed, quiet. But they are also deeply committed, passionate and respectful people.

When you see the Prince in a reading with the Knight of Disks, you could be looking at one of two situations – one, possibly a father and son combination (or something closely resembling this) may

Prince of Disks

Thoth Tarot

be reflecting. But you may also be looking at the growth of the boy into the man. The Knight is a balanced, materially stable individual, so if you saw these two with other Disk cards, you might conclude that this is the steady and dedicated progress of a young man toward his material goals.

Disks and Wands do not necessarily agree too well – the dynamism (and sometimes rashness) of Wands can tend to destabilise the more stolid Disks.

Yet sometimes, Wands can act as a breath of fresh air, blowing away caution and over-evaluation for the Disk. So cards such as the 5 or 10 of Wands, and sometimes the Ace, can act as irritants to the person represented by this Prince. But the 2, 3, 6 or 8 can offer an essential burst of confidence, energy, and willingness to communicate, which might otherwise be lacking.

Swords and Disks are surprisingly friendly, as Suits go. The sharp-eyed wit and intellect of the Swords, applied with the singular concentration of the Disk, can be absolutely undeniable in its force. This does, however point to a very specific danger for those men represented as the Prince of Disks. Such sharpness of wit, and solid determination, can sometimes also give rise to obsession, or mindless ruthlessness. The Ace, 2 and 6 of Swords are the most beneficial cards to appear for the Prince of Disks – they imply inner balance, the willingness and ability to make decisions, and the contact with the Higher Planes that breaks through the Disk earthiness when needed. However when we see combinations like high Swords with this card, we need to examine carefully whether perhaps that unfailing will is being applied in an immoral or wrong fashion.

Cups and Disks sometimes agree - and sometimes do not. The combination of earth and water can provide us with the ocean and the seabed, but it can also give us mud. Disks are emotional beings, despite some evidence to the contrary. However they tend to act upon their emotions, rather than drowning in them, or becoming immersed by them. So for instance, the Ace, 3, 9 and 10 of Cups are really happy cards to appear with this Prince – they indicate the start and continuance of deeply loving and strongly treasured relationships. However, the 4, 5, 7 and 8 tend to point toward at best, mud and murk, and at worst, the development of a victim mentality.

Of the Majors, the ones of outstanding significance are probably the Hermit – which indicates the necessary withdrawal the Prince needs in order to achieve renewal, and the Empress - because of her connections with family. Disks are all strongly rooted in the domestic round. They need rhythm and stability in these areas. The Empress embodies the principles at the heart of family life.

QUEEN OF DISKS

Queen of Disks

Thoth Tarot

This is a gentle card, which indicates a female who is primarily concerned with home and family. Strong keywords here are nurture, nourish and take care. When it appears with the Empress, it is often the younger members of the family who are commanding attention, or sometimes the process and concept of mothering.

When this card appears after a troubled and difficult period, it instructs the querent to be kind to themselves – reserves are quite low and need replenishing by gentleness and rest. Look for cards like Lust or the Sun to indicate recovery.

A lesser known aspect of the Queen of Disks can be revealed when she appears with either the Priestess or the Magician. This Queen is attuned to life. She has a deep love of the process of nature, and of the cycles which exist within existence itself. She engages in the practise of 'Right Attention' – putting the entire focus of her consciousness in the moment, and thereby creating magick. This aspect is emphasised when you see her appearing with either of these two magickal archetypes. She is interpreted as teaching this skill when she appears with the Hierophant. Look for other Courts to get some idea who will be the recipient of her wisdom.

If the Queen appears with cards like the 5 of Cups, or the 7 of Swords, the weaker side of her nature is beginning to emerge. Here she is no longer in touch with the power and force of her own energy. She has become bogged down in mundane matters and is unable to touch her soul. This starves her of nourishment. Whilst this Queen reacts more practically at times of emotional crisis than does, say, the Queen of Cups, when she does sink she sinks very low. Cards like the Devil would indicate that she is creating limitations which strangle her. The Tower would show an urgent need to break free, before events catch up with her. The 9 or 10 of Swords would be strong warning cards about self-harm.

In these circumstances you would be looking for strong Wands or Cups to indicate her eventual recovery. Again Lust or the Sun would be important here, as would the Universe, to suggest that she is passing through a cycle which will shortly come to an end.

If she appears with the Fool, there will probably be 'worry' cards about as well – the Queen does not deal well with risk-taking, preferring the reliable cycle to the sudden leap off the cliff. Expect to see the 5 of Disks, the 5 of Swords, or the Hanged Man to show this worry. But look also for 6's to confirm safe passage.

KNIGHT OF DISKS

This card most often represents an individual when it comes up in a reading. It
may relate to a man who has the qualities
of the Knight of Disks – quiet, determined, diligence which makes steady
progress toward goals. On the other hand,
it could represent the attitudes of a man
as he applies himself to his material and
career life.

The Knight of Disks can sometimes
become sluggish, bound up in the
mundane side of life, and this will lead to
frustration and dullness. Look for cards
like the 10 of Wands, the 8 of Swords, or
the 7 of Disks to warn of this. In this case,
he needs to break out and impress life
with his mark, or he will gradually begin
to lose his steady spirit.

Knight of Disks

Thoth Tarot

Whilst these men are prepared for the ups and downs of career life, they cope
poorly when there is indecision in these areas. The 2 of Disks, or again, the 7,
will indicate instability. He needs to be encouraged to act in these circumstances.

As a partner, the Knight of Disks will be loyal, deeply but privately passionate, and trustworthy. When family life is stable they are at their best. However they deal badly with emotional turbulence – they don't fit well with Cup-like people, for instance. If you read cards like the 9 or 10 of Swords, or the 7 or 8 of Cups around this card, there's a good chance the Knight will be in quite a lot of emotional trouble. Cards like Art, Adjustment and the 6 of Swords would be reassurances that things will gradually return to some semblance of normality.

If you feel that the card represents an attitude of mind rather than the core personality, it is worth looking for indications of why it is necessary for the person represented by the Knight to adopt this particular state of mind. Cards like the 5 of Disks might indicate that there are material difficulties and he needs to knuckle down and apply himself. Aces could mark the beginning of a new project which needs hard work and attention to detail.

A NOTE FROM ANGEL PATHS

First of all, we'd like to thank you for buying this book. Together with the people who support Angel Paths, you are keeping alive the idea that Jan devoted much of her life to.

We (Ellie and Graham) first met Jan in the late eighties when she was running face to face Tarot courses. Those courses went on to become the backbone for both this book and the website. And Jan went on from our Tarot teacher to become our friend. So, when she passed away in June 2019, she was already talking about passing the business to us when she retired. We respected her wish that the website and teaching lived on.

We've done what we can to honour her legacy and enable her words to reach as many people as possible.

With that in mind, we've done our best to tidy up the books, bring them into line with what readers would expect, while at the same time preserving the voice of Jan. Anyone who met her, either in real life or online, will know that she had a wicked sense of humour and a unique way with words and we hope this shines through in this book.

We've also kept the Card of the Day going. Every business day (in the UK) we pick a card, send it out via email, and post it on the Angel Paths Page on Facebook. It's a great learning experience to focus on one card at a time. If you wish to be added to the list, please go to the Angel Paths website and you can sign up from there.

As always, you're more than welcome to get in touch with corrections, comments, memories or anything else at admin@angelpaths.com.